W9-BCS-771

INTERGLACIAL

New and Selected Poems & Aphorisms

JAMES RICHARDSON

AUSABLE PRESS
2004

Cover art: Paul Klee, *Alter Klang,* 1925
236 (x 6); 38.1 x 37.8 cm
Oeffentliche Kunstsammlung, Basel

Design and composition by Ausable Press
The type is Granjon with Felix Titling.
Cover design by Rebecca Soderholm

Published by
AUSABLE PRESS
1026 HURRICANE ROAD
KEENE, NY 12942
www.ausablepress.org

Distributed to the trade by
CONSORTIUM BOOK SALES & DISTRIBUTION
1045 WESTGATE DRIVE
SAINT PAUL, MN 55114-1065
(651) 221-9035
(651) 221-0124 (FAX)
(800) 283-3572 (ORDERS)

The acknowledgments appear on page 251 and constititute a
continuation of the copyright page.

Library of Congress Cataloging-in-Publication Data

Richardson, James, 1950—
Interglacial : new and selected poems & aphorisms / James Richardson.
p. cm.
ISBN 1-931337-05-5 (trade cloth : alk. paper)—ISBN 1-931337-21-7 (trade paper : alk. paper)
1. Aphorisms and apothegms. I. Title.

PS3568.I3178I58 2004
811'.54—dc22

2004016235

In memory of
Cecil Y. Lang and Theodore Weiss,
my teachers

SELECTED POEMS & APHORISMS

Anyway   *1*

RESERVATIONS (1977)

In Touch   *5*
The Encyclopedia of the Stones: A Pastoral   *7*
The Dead   *19*
For October   *20*
Ashes   *22*
A Little Answer   *23*
On the Anniversary of Your Death   *24*
An Age   *25*

SECOND GUESSES (1984)

Your Way   *29*
Snow in May   *31*
Tastes of Time   *32*
The Fields Again   *34*
Another Spring   *35*
As One Might Have Said   *36*
Lines Separated by Years   *37*
To Odysseus on the Hudson   *38*
Ending an End   *41*
Second Guesses   *42*

Essay on Birds   *43*

True Confessions   *47*

Doppler Effects   *48*

Out of the Sun   *49*

Compositae   *53*

AS IF (1992)

In Fog   *57*

Splinters   *58*

Fruit Flies   *59*

Blue Heron, Winter Thunder   *62*

For Now   *65*

How It Ends   *67*

Signs, Signs!   *68*

The Mind-Body Problem   *69*

Locusts   *70*

My Mistake   *71*

Cat Among Stones   *72*

Post-Romantic   *73*

A Pause   *74*

A Measure   *75*

Out of School   *76*

Early Violets   *78*

Marigolds   *79*

At First, At Last   *80*

As If Ending   *93*

HOW THINGS ARE (2000)

How Things Are: A Suite for Lucretians   97
Afterword   117
Under Water
   The Flood   *120*
   Little Bridge   *121*
   Salvage   *122*
   Undersong   *122*
   Letter from One of Many Worlds   *123*
   River Sunset   *124*
   Water Music   *125*
   The Water As It Was   *126*
   The Dreaming-Back   *126*
   The Bridge Again   *127*
Poison   *128*
Defense   *129*
My Young Carpenter   *130*
A Disquisition upon the Soul   *131*
Nine Oaks   *132*
Mothy Ode   *133*
For the Birds   *136*
Through Autumn   *141*

VECTORS: *Aphorisms & Ten-Second Essays* (2001)   *158*

INTERGLACIAL: *New Poems and Aphorisms* (2004)

MONSTER MOVIES

Spellbound   *181*

My Godzilla   *182*

Collateral Damage   *183*

The Poor   *184*

Monster Movies   *185*

End of the World   *187*

World News Tonight   *188*

In Black and White   *189*

Still Life with Moving Figure   *190*

Virgin and Son   *191*

All the Ghosts   *192*

Frictions   *194*

SF   *196*

Ghost Story   *198*

Death   *199*

HALF MEASURES

Firstcomers   *203*

Desire   *203*

Again   *204*

Paused   *204*

Recall   *204*

Boulder   *205*

Valediction   *205*

House   *205*

Could Not   *206*

Found   *206*

Purpose   *206*

Lunar   *207*

Household Tips   *207*

Cliff   *207*

Capital   *207*

E Pluribus Unum   *208*

Flock   *208*

Any Port   *208*

Sparrows   *208*

Reunion   *209*

History   *209*

Relativistic Effects   *209*

The Cardinals   *210*

Writer   *210*

The Book of Everything   *210*

Ancient   210

Parallel Lines   *211*

Gravitas   *211*

Form   *211*

Ratio of Volume to Surface Area   *211*

VECTORS 2.0:
More Aphorisms & Ten-Second Essays   *214*

LATECOMERS

Early Snow   *229*

Latecomers   *231*

Early and Late   *235*

In Snow   *236*

Evening Prayer   *241*

Another End of the World   *242*

Late Snow   *243*

Interglacial   *244*

Epilogue in Snow   *245*

Acknowledgments and Notes   249

ANYWAY

The way an acre of starlings towers and pours
rapidly through itself, a slipping knot,
landing so few feet down the furrows (the whole skywriting
like a secret no one knows they have given away)
is one of those breathtaking wastes
(sun and the seeds they feed on being others)
in which something senseless, even selfish, absurdly magnified,
becomes grandeur (love is another).
Sometimes the flock, banking in unison,
vanishes an instant, like a sheet of paper edge-on
(a secret, anyway, is the illusion
confessing it would make a difference).
I watched this happen once—two seconds, hours—
till I understood no kindness, not a shadow or stone.
And they did not come back,
though I waited all evening (and it was you
I waited for). Though the sky turned black.

RESERVATIONS (1977)

IN TOUCH

When for no reasons but his own the silent cat
throttled your song,
I buried you in the tone-deaf garden,
alone, as I thought.

But when the shimmering catch
of sun unrolled—
blazon of corn, flourish
of feathery fennel,
deep liquid melon trill—
you are up,
and holding level in the level air
inconceivable wings!

At the first defeat,
the unutterable concentrations, the bullet grace,
disband.
The blood darkens, the eyes crowd,
the body like a vast party breaks up
into smaller and more passionate nights.

Bird, bright metal, renegade nerve, whom
no one ever touched, you now
touch openly,
and in the long and careless sun
unfold and loll and glow.

Far far down everywhere,
where even the light is far apart, the very eye
invisibly huge, matter waits in endless lines
to find out what it is.
Into the mindlessly small

the mind may not enter; nor touch
into the untouchable.

So we are just passing through
each other, deep embraces like a bullet's
kiss and ricochet; or say
we hold as waves
seize, hold, O never hold, the shore.

The willing, nervous living flash and fly.
The stubborn dead relent, and die. And die
into us, craggy water that our memories
labor to admit. They are ours

when they are not their own.
They walk into the grave, and do not stop,
but break, join hands, and breed
with stone, and slug, and light, and dandelion.

THE ENCYCLOPEDIA OF THE STONES:
A PASTORAL

1
They do not believe in the transmigration of souls.
They say their bodies will move
as leaves through light.

Everything would be perfect if the atoms
were the right shape and did not fall down.

2
They resent being inscribed
as if they could not remember,
but they congratulate us on the wisdom
of using them to mark graves.

3
Sand makes them nervous.

4
They perceive the cosmos as the interior
of a mighty stone.
At night this is perfectly clear.

5
Long ago
they began to give of their light
to build what we now call the moon.
It was almost finished.

6
Tradition says they were the paperweights of a lord
whose messages rotted beneath them.
So they think hard.

The old remember being flowers,
but the young ridicule them and remember fire.

7
Some say they were prayers
until they lost confidence;
others, the ashes
of the shrieking cold.

8
This is their heroic myth:
One afternoon the great stone set out.

It is not over.

9
They are unable to perceive moths.

10
They have a dream, but it is taking
all of them all time
to imagine it.

11
It is the same with their dance,
which has gone on since the beginning
without the repetition of a step.

12
They have computed the human life span
to the nearest hundred years.

13
Knowing them to be fond of games, I asked
why they did not arrange themselves
according to the constellations, but they said

Look.

14
Under water they hear each other
and glow.

15
After a long drought, break one open.
It may be wet from the rain
of the fortieth day, and still springing back
from the terrible pressure of Noah's foot.

16
They are fond of each season in its turn,
regretting only brevity.

They suspect this world was not made for them.

17
No hand is slow enough, really,
to catch a stone:
the long forest burns
and grows and burns before the jostled stone
like roiled water settles clear again
to its root and its prayer and its home.

18
They recognize everything.

19
They suppose that if they could forget enough
they would become stars.

20
One of them is counting the days,
but they go so fast he cannot stop
to tell us how many.

21
Stone (stōn), noun. Originally a verb meaning
to illumine blackness, later
to hold without touching, or
to be capable of all things. In modern,
and less felicitous, speeches,
Indo-European, for example,
to thicken or compress.
Still later, as we know.

22
Here is another of their stories:
One stone.
Like the others it is characterized
by control of plot and fidelity to the real.

23
The progress of the stone:

Primevally—a sun unto itself.
In the next age—a bend in moonlight.
Failing this—a cauldron of teeth.
Still later, pitted and harried—a dawn of iron.
In time, our time, a recalcitrant image
in a bed away from the dream.

24
They are experimenting with sex
but are still waiting for the first ones to finish.

25
They are attracted by bright lights
(especially white and blue)
at the rate of one inch per millennium.

They have large and obscure purposes
expressed as continental drift.

26
Fossils: monuments
to their tolerance. Eons
upon eons of surrender
bring a flower to bed with stone.

There is another theory: one stone
remembers one thing—
vividly.

27
They have rings
like trees, a kind of consummation,
growing from inside almost as fast
as they are eroded.

28
When it is unbearably clear,
the stones have taken a deep breath.

29
They have much to teach us
of what we should already know.

30
They place a high value on wit
and refuse to believe it is because they are afraid.

31
They think they eat,
but because they have never been hungry
the question is purely academic.

32
They grumble at the consequences
of leaving no stone unturned.

33
They are fond of the phrase *after all.*

34
They never had much use for birds
even before the crisis.

35
When I describe to them how we see a shooting star,
they say *That is how you look to us.*

When I tell them how they look to me,
they are elated and describe in turn
something I have never seen and do not understand.

36
Another day dawns and the stones
labor incessantly until they have
filled it with darkness.

37
Some of their favorites: October,
salt, flowers, 10 P.M., starfish,
Paul Klee, stories, waiting, the moon.

38

You know that the sky is blue
from the accumulated breath of stones,
or will, next time you are asked.

39

When they stare at themselves too long
they become diamonds.

40

Sometimes in the intense light
they are seen to quake.
And they say *Never mind,*
sun, old burrower
into our dreams.

41

They do not understand the difference
between dying and just going away.
When I walk home they weep,
but not for long.

42

They have been called the eyes
of the lost angels,
and it is true they remember
great lights, and a fall,
and that they seem to be waiting
for something to go away.

43
Here is another one of their stories:
*One day the great stone went out
and never returned.*

They do not understand this one,
and it is therefore of dubious authenticity.

44
They are very clever at imitation.

45
They question the parable of Perseus and Medusa,
saying that mirrors, of all things,
would be no help.

46
They cannot tell the living from the dead.
Be careful to clarify your position.

47
The success of unbearable intimacy:
two stones,
the one to the windward finally
the more smooth.

48
I told them my favorite story:
One day.

They liked it except for the
surprise ending.

49
They know the infinitesimal ways
to the center of peach and oyster,
cherry, brain and heart.

50
They are continually astonished
at the thousands of ways we have invented
to say *I am dying.*

51
They do not mind lying in the sun,
especially when there is no choice.

52
They call themselves the abbreviation
of distance.

53
They have a proverb: *Absurdity
is marvelous, but you get hungry an hour later.*

I reply *But that is what it is for.*

54
Knowing and unknowing never love,
but form the maelstrom within the stone.

55
They have something they will say to us,
but they are revising and revising.

56
They think of the whole day
as sunset.

57
Along the margin of the lake,
stones in a simple line, taking account
of the shouts of generations of lilies,
are polishing the desperate poverty of life
into an opulence beyond all conception of light.

58
This whole encyclopedia reminds me of a stone.
It does not remind them of anything.

When they say *That reminds me of a stone,*
 it means they will not
say anything else for a long time.

59
I asked *How can we keep you out of the fields?*
They said *Give us a place of our own.*

This was not like them.

60
They are never disappointed
because they expect nothing.

61
It is possible they would die for us
if they could find a reason.

62
They try to forget,
but their sadness for the flowers will be told
again and again,
though it seems I am no longer the one.

63
I say *How do you get to the river?*
They say *It will come.*

THE DEAD

There is still the smell of them,
bitterer than they were, like snuffed candles,
and the skins of cold they shed
tremble between the stars.

Everywhere the imprint of their eyes! The path
turns with them. Their gestures return,
subdued, an Indian summer.
I bring a few flowers.

Why ask what is to be loved,
now there is nothing.
The question is who am I
who still walk with them.

FOR OCTOBER

On the thirty-first of your allotted days,
you wound along the ridge dividing
the poor from the hopeful, wading high
in the last gasp of tangled undergrowth.

You plowed down the slope, struggled
up over the crest, stumbled again into sight,
taking nothing, seeing no one, as if
disappearance were your only purpose.

No one knew you were anything
but the meter reader, jiggling doorknobs,
frightening the darkness of basements
with your heavy flash, noting carefully

what we had used, what left behind.
But I saw you record the stillness
of cats shining in the high grass like streams,
praise the infinite readiness

of weeds, savor the rumble of
imminent frost. I saw you say good-bye,
good-bye to the homes, as if they were
rows of squat, tenacious greens

you had helped to plant. You with tang
of smoke and windfalls, you
quietly revealing after the months
in disguise, before the months

in the guise of honesty. Everyone
likes you, but you need no help to
be what you are. You our best moment,
you of the grave and terrible children.

Summer kept loving us. We tried
to give ourselves away. Now we wheel,
fling off desire, bearing down
like the wind under the door.

Later, what we still need
finds us. Someone looks at a watch. It's dark.
Taking the shortcut, you outrun destruction,
not having, now, to be careful of the gardens.

ASHES

Into the gradual evening
we wake, having only arrived
in our half of light, where dim pines,
wind-visited, seethe and snap,
but no one calls fire.

Though there is burning, burning
of a cool but tortuous kind,
and the sky flickers, burning,
and the first drops count the leaves

like a dissolving clock, and wind
down the flue to speak,
with old ashes, of bitterness.

Of bird light turned low in the nest, the powdery
moth driven under his haven;
of us with our vast
no place to be.

And it seems that this day will go on,
parallel lines never touching,
two stones in the rain.

A LITTLE ANSWER

Light swaying
and straightening, like reeds. It has been
everywhere. The waves
sidling up the shore are strung with it,
the shells eaten through with it.
If I bend I will spill
a great blaze.

Gulls, the cry
of nights hung out to whiten. Sand,
what of the sun has slowed. Wind,
what has already happened
remembering us. There is no such thing
as solitude, though we
are what comes of it.

ON THE ANNIVERSARY OF YOUR DEATH

September. Kids drift back to school,
rigid and sweaty in premature
plaids and wool.

The house is settling.
Beams speak out of turn. A rudderless moth
thuds in the shade,

and you move in
with the deference of dust
to crowd this emptiest of months.

You're twenty-one. You've grown.
O, stay.

AN AGE

It is when
you have labored all winter
to prove you are content, and in

your quick, cold sleep
do not hear the rain,
that you wake

astonished in the glare
of ice, the world worn smooth
as your eye—

distinction lost, all
that rugged good
glossed over.

And you walk tight-shouldered, broken-
kneed along the shine that wants you
split like a wishbone.

Frictionless, we do not come
to much. Nothing strikes,
warms, gets stuck, parts slowly—

so you do not know where you are,
flaring off,
air mooring air.

The ice has climbed
to disembody everything. Out
on a limb, it mocks

the gutless duck four months amazed
in the high shrubs. It comes
to glare through the sockets, to wedge

the bill open, to freeze
the radial array of feathers splashed
against cold shot.

And you have come down
to peer through the narrowing hole of yourself.
O, the conflagration of purity! You can

hardly see you thinning
into the white burn centimeters
above the fiery path.

It is when
you have labored all winter, called
one thing another, and all

by your own name,
that the light gets hold of the world, and shakes,
and shakes you away, and only

the love you need
gathers, colors,
steadies itself, takes strenuous root,

SECOND GUESSES (1984)

YOUR WAY

This is the last month you can follow
the dry runnel's long diminution
a mile upstream through remnants of a wood
just broad enough for both ends of a robin.

It's easy now—skirting the backyards
of new colonials or old split-levels
raised starkly on their knobs as faces
white and surprised in severe haircuts.

But now their night-dressed Occupants might marvel
at your hike in chancy weather, gazes
heavying your shoulder as the blinds zip shut.
Then—or sooner—you'd wonder why you bothered,

and mumble, obligingly, to the seething pines
that you'd come just for the silver-brown of fields
so yearned-at by motel art you forget
that it, if anything, is real.

Up close, it's like a streak of monarch's wing dust.
Step back, and it's the shapelessness of hills,
distinguishing indistinctness, but mostly
it's like having nothing to liken things to.

Go now, though maybe I've neglected something
of barbed wire, or a conduit under the pike,
or the simple fact that scarcely a day
runs straight enough to get—nowhere.

But now, if ever. In a rain or two,
the bed will suck you to the knees; you'll stroke
through an ounce of midges to the cubic foot,
bred in that gully the sun blinds with weeds.

Then no one pioneers it but the neighbor kids
on the first August day someone thinks *School,*
with helmets, canteens, something like a machete,
and pockets of cookies ground to damp meal.

You'll hear them thrashing home through evening.
Their voices, straggling, immediate as smoke,
land everywhere, so that you think
of faith ubiquitous as gravity—

but is it more, or less, than you
that they've believed? You'll feel an adolescent body
shift inside yours, loosely packed, and have
to convince yourself of what midsummer teaches

about the getting and keeping of streams.
That, barring extraordinary efforts,
you get just one thing or the other—
where the water came from, or the water.

SNOW IN MAY

I don't know how we weathered
the lilacs' collision with snow.
While that backward front
stalled over Boston, jays launched

out on two days at once. Two days
clashed, snowed, stilled,
each cornice, twig, instant
distinct with chill,

and sharp in memory
as if there the past broke off.
Unheard of, so new, we tried to believe
spectacular cold could clear

what we owned and owed. The evening
swept in particles
across the walks, and snow
touched here, there, our unreadiness.

TASTES OF TIME

. . . vegetable love should grow
Vaster than empires, and more slow.
—Marvell

Nothing could taste the way coffee smells
or red pears look. The tongue gives up
on dogwood smashed by wind,

and watching you bend over peppers
snapping in oil, I want you
all the way to the beginning, when you are

not even memory, but a photo
of yourself at six, only the small face
visible through high corn dense as a broom.

If you could grate the October sky
into short fibers, hardly blue close up,
like a handful of water, that

would be a radish, cool, austere,
as near to nothing as we can grasp.
One step redder, heartier,

a crab apple is the yard
I summered in, where vast cecropias
haunt bowls of honey and beer.

Who can distinguish these plants
from the spaciousness of lives? There is one
jostling the rows with desires

we did not know were ours.
Less dream than hardiness, not wholly
sweet, but whole in stems and leaves,

it is the weed slipping fine blue rays
through walk and porch, where the flags
or the hours do not quite meet.

THE FIELDS AGAIN

Years back, my plunge for viceroys slowed
in waist-high musk. One of those
green, lace-winged flies
smeared in the chase, I guessed.

In the field today, that scent—
part camphor, part sweat—
suddenly remembered me,
so I turned, asking *Who.*

Now that names are permitted
it was yarrow.
I look for what small shame,
years later, might have shocked

pastward through boy and net,
maddening whirligigs on the pond
so the day, tall among reeds,
shivered and went dark.

Why does such memory vanish,
or well up, heated bodily,
from an opened bed? It seems that we
are almost accidentally alive—

I do not even now smell half
the lucky, meaningless
distinctions of green, or love in you
more than old, old wrong can recognize.

ANOTHER SPRING

Moths thick as swallows
softly batter the porch light.
The magnolia
swarms with luminous darkness.

Now the innocent faithlessness of May
spills. Breathing, all
I have heard of beautiful pain
hurts and is beautiful.

Each hour demands
a different happiness. This one
is easy: to darken,
more naked, like bark after rain.

AS ONE MIGHT HAVE SAID

May, and O might,
updraft and spin of blossom, can
all our furl, human,
untwist for this ridiculous
rose-must and white—in love with trees?
What evolutions
crossed here—did ur-man
blow through cleft trunks,
that throw and wind-fear of his loins
cached now in the genes, so we
in the dazzle and torque of petals
say, say against
ourselves, *I have walked in the churning
heart of a god?*

LINES SEPARATED BY YEARS

Under the window, a hare
chews hyacinths. Imagine
the sweet fat, the violet eyes.

What intricacies
of desire the simple
body can enclose.

Let us scorn the dead.
Of our night
they have left no record.

It took centuries of dressing
to make this nakedness.

TO ODYSSEUS ON THE HUDSON

Midstream, midsummer, what reaches you
from shore is a freak of the wind:
one word snatched by like a leaf,
silence, seconds of cicadas'
shrill acceleration. That way
gods spoke—suddenly, once. You recall
smooth, loose-jointed hostels
where the windows, dried by noon, dove shut.

There was somewhere to go.
You half-remember
the spell you started with:
immortality, peculiar
tyranny of youth.
Free, you'd fit anywhere,
but anywhere's an island
left by raising your eyes
through the transparent, early moon.

Haven after haven, stewing oxen
in their own stomachs over fires of bone,
you felt your sacrifice
seep through bedrock
into the mouth of the right god.
The sheets were stiff with salt. The nymphs,
each loveliest, began to merge
in the anonymity of want.

Yearly, the hazards grew younger.
Not wanting their lazy,
tidal affection, you closed your eyes
by thinking of their trouble still to come,
and imagined yourself

hulk among children, dwarf among monsters—
not old yet, but untranslatable,
grotesque and smooth as driftwood.
You learned that for their adoration
you would waste your life explaining.

Second time through, your story,
long enough to unroll from Troy,
held friends you recognized
who still weren't yours. In the end
you loved one who already knew:
Circe, with her spell of the real.
She was right; your friends were pigs.
She showed the faint dead
bargaining for your blood, and dreamed
more sea, companions devoured,
and Ithaca, sharp coast
you pretended to remember.

Glass doors opened into rooms,
wind-grayed, lightened for summer.
A dazzling horizon breathed
under white sheets in the cool
well-made bed. Penelope? A myth.
It was Circe, your home after all.

Hard old lovers, miscellaneous
as provisioned houses, you brought
two of everything and made up history.
Together you invented
the bedpost filed from an olive trunk,
and called the twenty years of accident ·
waiting, all lost youths being the same.

Days broaden and thin behind
like wakes. You begin to see the past
from above and to the right, watching yourself
on firm beds or sieved through reefs
as only another could have,
or a god—the one you sensed
as gray sea first, then a murmur
years later hardening,
like the basaltic root of the island,
into words you said to her.

ENDING AN END

Up like wet thumbs for the breeze,
we listened for the blue Hudson

cutting and soothing the core.
Now, even that canyon

of a summer seems to digress.
Heal-all and dayflower

interrupted the asphalt.
I too constructed ruins:

how could we disappoint when no one
knew we were alive!

Nothing will ever be so large
as that river, so small as those weeds.

Maybe this life life-scale was what you saw,
as if longing cleared and broadened

into light, and we met just this
lightly, as mirrors believe rooms.

SECOND GUESSES

There's hardly a story. At five,
embarrassingly few reasons
for being so tired, even habit
wouldn't keep us in place.
In the merciless, low light,
cotton frayed, wool shone,
every scrape and nick
blazed, every delta of grit.
Even our bodies seemed shabby
as old pillows leaking
feathers and odor of scalp
that we'd sleep on all our lives.

Then the sun got worse, dust
fired down in angelic ranks,
and we lay back as the room went blind.
White heat glared through my hands
and squeezed lids, with a red
so garish, so human, only nature
could get away with it.
Fingers groped into my fingers, hot
spines threaded my spine, and I
was a miracle, I guess, heart
thrusting light.
           O, I admit
I'm back, the same old hulk. By now,
no vision would change me,
even if its radiance weren't borrowed
from a poster of Greek islands
or somewhere in the *Paradiso*.

But that second flashed the life
before birth, when, at the sun's core,
we dreamed these three years I know best
as slowly as they would happen
until just then, when the room
refocused piece by piece
and we rose for dinner, clattering
among white plates
in the modest labor of being together.

Nothing divine, you see. No voice
told us anything about the future,
except that there is none
and we are free. Life has
already happened. Now that it's over
we can talk it over,
and do again what we liked.

ESSAY ON BIRDS

It is not their parenthetical
remarks of color—jay and cardinal
brilliant after cold rain—
but their continual impossibility
that befriends us. When the grackles
settled on the leafless orchard
like black, early fruits, you wondered
whether it *could* have happened.

Nothing explains the vertigo
of their arrival: as if
their solitaires and broken flocks
were the wrong words for what we try
to say, and when they ring us, feeding
at their inviolable distance,
they trace out what we mean
by tip of the tongue, back of the mind.

How their bones blow, hollowed for flight,
or what they see, threshing our gutters
with their hard wings,
we might remember, but not how
they pulse along the Mississippi
flyway, hearing the moon
slide both oceans on pale floors,
or how Polaris, nearer than the brain,
throngs their wings with colors beyond violet
they name Soar, Death and Call.

Coasting the magnetic field,
they sense the magmas,
aquifers it darkens through
as vast clouds moored in the planet.

It is hard to liken shades
of lodestone glancing on the nerves
to what we know—falling, perhaps,
or the reluctance of earth turning over—
but we may feel them in the way
we know the time precisely until asked—
as desire too early to be desire.

For what we see in birds
is how much help there is for acts
too simple to be labor. Chickadees
natter on the railing, spaced
with laughable precision,
and buoyed with the good fame
of symmetries before love
where we are pure and possible.
With such knowledge, we might
never move, but maybe
the present divides, for even they
flick and glide in finding
the same place, which is never still.

Clocking the planets, the stiffening
of sea and leaf, they must sense each second
as a stitch in a seam.
This is what you wanted to know—
merely, always, that we happen
as things do happen,
that you could touch life
wholly, continuously
as the slight burn of kite string
paying out through two fingers.
But they do not need to understand

or tell us, so we take
their mistake for friendship when,
drunk on turned berries, they swoop
giddily near, like large, harmless bees.

History confirms
it's hard not to think of them as messengers.
Once an ashen sparrow
dropped from the flue, and the three
billion-year relay of protoplasm
passed to you, who could still
read there, garbled in the genes,
what made you raise the rigid body
up to the sun, thinking, for a second,
your hand might come down empty.

TRUE CONFESSIONS

In my unwritten novel we would hear
the evening paper, blunt on the door,
untuck for the wind's disassembly
page after page in bottomless recession.

We'd be exes perhaps, chapters of absence
having slipped us from old explanations
into something more comfortable:
stellar distance. But you know how it was.

Pairing truths, we leveled with each other.
I don't remember any of the facts,
not one—just your wrist's occasional
so-what, like the turning of a page.

In love, or less, unsaying hands
are freer and more certain than our hold
on exactly what real secrets are.
Not the day but its reticence endures.

For it's disquietingly easy to confess
fear and undistinguished shame,
as if they hadn't quite happened to us,
but nearby, like accidents, or rain.

DOPPLER EFFECTS

One day the universe's long sigh outward
catches. For the moment our red-shifted stars
shift blue, we shall see things as they are,

stilled, in final relation: the maple
caved where the west wind fed,
and a starling's fear on a wire.

I swear in this middle year of my life
I heard the night brake, and a kerchief
slide in a drawer, so I woke

in this morning one jay narrower,
to a jay's cry one tone higher,
and began that blue and backward fall.

Regret precedes its cause. I reach at last
the love betrayed, leave
as I came, untouching her,

and see from that other side what we had done
cleared of time—not undone, but remembered
causeless, bluer, irresponsible.

OUT OF THE SUN

... *the soul*
Remembering how she felt, but what she felt
Remembering not ...

—Wordsworth

When your postwar Plymouth
rattled up to our eternal practice,
and you vaulted the fence,
we'd drift down from the wildness
memory does not hold, still half sky
from shagging day-long flies.

Sweat-suited, someone's father,
you'd bawl *Men!* Did the future press
like a strange body?
Not then—we hurtled in
at what fraction of lightspeed
white sneakers could attain.

At our diamond by the dump,
gulls shrieked contradiction to the mounds.
The rich, high smell seemed speed burned off
from dust over third, stung thighs,
your fungoes dropping
like Jap Zeroes out of the sun.

All those years fine down
to one day, in summer. I toed the rubber
once. Just once,
I idled to the bench in Mantle's
broken-kneed trot, head bowed
in imaginary pride or pain.

Double-time! The small team sprinted in
through the day large from repetition,
and the teens, fingers just touching,
wandered into the grove for their stiff love
according to the movies, true
for all we knew.

Fanned, picked off, we reconciled with failure
out on the dump, where time spoke all at once
our lives, if we could guess the order.
A stove caved in a Chevy. Bedsprings
shivered on a nest of dolls.
Disastrous freedoms still adhere

like a more transparent air
to junk I smuggled home.
Shelved, unlikely, unaccountable
as someone else's memories,
it poses the solitude
of the blinding past.

Weren't we wise then?
While you sang in the devoted roar
of the mower, we fingered medals
in your shirt drawer, whispering
Pacific islands—
Okinawa, where the Duke cries
when the underage Iowa GI
flings against a wall at last
in the perfect diving catch.

It seemed so natural,
that courage without reasons,
like the lives that ran
without us, in the suspension of gravity
I still mistake for grace.

But your one war story was *No stories.*
We straddled our bikes while you
doused the car. Pail after pail
flashed on the chrome, darkened the drive.

And I never moved
because there were too many ways
to go, not one odd life
like yours, in khakis with sagging pockets
and blunt, dark fingers
screwing a hose tight or fishing for keys,
facts you have receded from
that I loved but could not say.

So you passed, from what now
seems inattention. I could not see
the patient white sleeves, shaved blush
of the married to work, or how much
of child's death, angry bed
converged in your flawless swing.

Only now I look out
from under the scorepad shading your eyes,
feel that grin tighten as waves
of leaping uniforms break at your feet,
half worship, half assault,
though nothing I know is on your mind.

I would lose you,
memory vague, the team photo
hopelessly overexposed—but you rise
in me, before your face or name,
as high light, kind gravity, the body hurling.

It is good to have back there
the indestructible leisure

of being so entirely wrong, needed now
again and again. Good that your jalopy
noses up to the field as we squint for you
through the glaring windshield
and the nine balls in the air
drop in ragged sequence.
As you were! As we are.

COMPOSITAE

It's autumn. Are there more of us,
or is it just the illusion
of weakened gravity and doubling wind—
more flocks of letters lifting from the desk,
more rapid hikes to smooth the loose paths down.

Squirrels drilling, frantic, random,
are the old rumor confirmed
by wildflowers hitching the county road.
More of *them,* but all
one hard family, *Compositae*
(aster, goldenrod, and thistle),
except the small umbrellas of wild carrot,
touchingly precise, but useless now.

More rooms and wools, more fires
and darkness behind them. More
of our one kind—the wanting.
What flies is starling; what stays, brown.
And all thrown sideways as the planet corners
on the thrill we thought was death, but is
miles and miles of what we failed to be!

AS IF (1992)

IN FOG

Sometimes, early and cold, you stumble
into the land's confusion
of tract and interstate with cracked harrow
and with fog, and with fog again.

The meadows, deepening, go stoneless.
Head-on two cars,
in a blaze, transpose.
There is nothing that is not everywhere.

And the jet extending through the fog like fog,
surrounding drone,
and the trill arriving as a blur
of any bird or other than bird,

and the houses, fogbound, that digress
in vague contrition,
smoking upward, flooding the road:
you take them in with a breath,

and breathe out feather, rock, and engine,
lightly, lightly, for the fog avers
that to forget and begin again
is not different from going on and on.

Just by looking, or not looking too hard,
you can love anything, says the fog.
You can gaze straight into the sun,
grayed and mild, now, as a moon.

Shrewd is unkind, I chose nothing, it sighs,
louder and louder as the day
takes hold, and all the years,
and that it was wrong becomes clearer and clearer.

SPLINTERS

They must have streamed like thistledown
from that first deep splinter,
surfacing in the scar, and yearly
further up my side, and fainter.

I thought I could feel them, childishly,
school along my heart, or rise
as starlings shearing in crosswinds
of November, my inner land.

A failing cry in the clouds, the tremor
of the frost-iris ringing the moon
may be night migration, or their slide,
translucent, over the mind's eye.

In the flush, the tenderness, the shying,
suddenly something, microscopic—
lost, often, in the tweezing,
so I wonder *Was that it, was there anything?*

If they are new ones, as I am told,
I never remember getting them,
though I think often in this season
of lengthening walks *On this path here,*

or there, I must have. When love alters,
for all your watching, isn't it sudden,
though no matter where you look,
or how far back, you find and find the reason?

FRUIT FLIES

Then in a wailful choir the small gnats mourn . . .
— Keats

Though you cellar it in the shrewdest cold,
airtight, and without the faintest print
or contusion, thinking of nothing,
and lounge at sundown by a golden window,
they will descend, as if remembering,
on whatever is turning.

You will hear in a drowse their breezeless
pervasion of your screens all evening
and not know whether darkness
or a hand-size swarm of them conspires
to disturb, in your hand, the focus of a pear.

And then, because your noticing makes more,
they are everywhere, a graininess in vision,
as if you had stayed up past your usual hour,
or some memory had persisted all year
as hands near your hand, an air on the air.

What you have spared all year, unwillingly,
they love to the stone, a live annihilation,
and when nothing is left whole they settle,
uncloyed, over your spills, or concentrate
in a clouded spoon.
                         Or shade, when your eyes must close,
your moist lids, or the little bridge of your lips,
and behind your ear the finger of cologne,
and everywhere you open, the sweet fluids.
                                        So close at last
you cannot say where the delve and pause

59

of your breathing ends, and they begin,
something like passion, only helpless and weary,
something like darkness, only rife and wild,
body that fills your body to the eyes.

AS A GHOST

Somehow in a November fever
to see you once more as you were
before our life—no bitterness
of mine taken into your face—
I was a ghost, all eyes
as you hastened from room to room
or, reading under a narrow light,
muttered to yourself, alone.
What came over you
was my breathing, like an untouched glass,
loss, my alcohol.

Something silken and unshy
that you might draw, pointing your foot,
up the sheer of your calf and thigh,
I rose on you, I rounded you
with water's faint
lift of your breasts, with the wind's lift,
spreading your hair.

And I was lost forever
unless I could remember,
as a ghost, and faithless,
what I had to remember
before your mind changed, or the windows grayed,
or the phone rang and I heard you speak of me.

BLUE HERON, WINTER THUNDER

All up and down the coast that November,
driving or reading, I heard it, over my shoulder,
tinnier than summer's, winter thunder.
Was it the first ever or, disbelieving,
had I forgotten the sound, resounding stone,
that hollowed me, that caught me rising—
brief shame, a truck of wind, a clearing?

Every evening, bridging the horizons,
one of those hours-long clouds, oily and bronze,
that as a child . . . that I still think are great fish—
or thoughts I cannot have for decades yet—
cruised over, soundless, or larger than hearing,
or in the astonishment of congratulation,
and I breathed thickly, safe at my depth.

We looked up, always, into the sourceless brightness
of like becoming more like, of days blending together.
One dawn, or every one, leaves broke into our room
with a strange slowness, a live glow.
Once or a thousand times we turned
sideways, passing in the narrow hall,
and you repeated: what was so true I won't remember.

How many times was it April? Rod in a soft arch,
I dragged my lure repeatedly over drowned brush
where I felt, as if it were in me down in the darkness,
the tremble, the soft mouth, nearly a strike,
though I was surely worrying the bottom.
How provocative hope is, how querulous!
And here is another thing I cannot say slowly enough.

How, when my gaze stood hard on the sky,
a cloud slipped, spring broke, the lake opened—
no the lake *had* opened, cryless,
and there was mountainous invisibility, or wings
blue-gray at first, then lucid: sky before I could point.
And I *did* point, though I was alone.
Or: where I pointed, wings rose, I was alone.

Thunderously. But was there thunder,
staggering the day, and did November
show for an instant through that shaken April,
chill, dark rising, then for a moment, stars?
Blue heron, the books said. Habits, ordinary.
Wingspread? Miles less than in imagination.
No thunder, I read and read. No consolation.

November, the jet blew up on our slope and burned.
That's what the papers said, that's what I must have seen.
But when God asks: I heard the crash first and saw—
as if I'd been pouring gas that backflashed—
the plane, still high, already on fire
with the future. I turned and there was no one there.
I turned, and there was no one there for years.

I still look up. The furnace ignites, rumbling,
in the blue, early dark. A blow of leaves.
Not swiftly, *suddenly* that heron vanishes—
as if offscreen. The flash not lightning,
the long resounding *longer* of no thunder.
Because you are out of time
you shall wake again and again and not remember.

As if your face, our story, as if day after day
were the sheen in someone's hair. Shift, not there.
And, sky darkening, I looked past my reflection
down into turbid waters, phosphorescent limbs,
pleasure to water, pain to dark water,
and there was the night, or the day in negative:
among the slim white trunks, white rain, white rain.

FOR NOW

The doorless barn holds nothing
out or in.
What you hear, if you listen,
is your listening.

Motionless the pruned limb,
half way down,
the heat of the blade still on it,
the resinous tang.

Soundlessly a swallow's
contained fright
crosses a sill forever,
part dark, part in light,

and, urgent once, the stone,
which the spell allows
to hang like a small gray moon,
forgets to follow.

And the storming child is absorbed,
mid-leap, mid-fall,
whether in rage or remorse
you cannot tell.

Fantastic, lengthened out,
his cry or call,
like a record winding down,
has deepened, inaudible.

Would they hear it, if they turned,
those lovers, turning,
on the point of a declaration,
coming or going?

All morning for a cheek to warm,
an hour to unclose an eye.
Is it joy, is it pain that lingers,
or surprise

at the stillness spreading in rings
from their last words,
endlessly *For now,*
whatever they wished for.

Beauty is clear in the instant;
weakness or strength, in season.
There is no time here to remember
patience, patience,

or to turn, or to think of turning
from your years at the window,
gazing deeply into this letter
you have received, or written.

HOW IT ENDS

Wind and a weakness, dandelion
letting go
through a rift in summer. Someone imagines
loving the cold.

Out of the clouds the slant wish,
one color—
dust on the pond, your breath
closing a mirror.

SIGNS, SIGNS!

That summer, phenomenal creatures.
I struck a match: white-eyed,
a rat surged in the john.
A fan of wings,
staticky, strobe-clear,
rippled my brow and was gone.
That summer of blackouts and thunder
I glanced up. Quick
on the glass, two catbirds
joined like spills. It was dark,
it was late: my book
swam and I turned the page.
Signs, signs! Was it death, was it love
accelerating past,
near miss, or someone else's?
Or, after all, no secret,
but life, so long in the hearing—
like a stunning, thunderous
train you've stopped for,
lifelong, at a crossing.

THE MIND-BODY PROBLEM

A blast-off, a butte, a downpour,
preposterous, of chains and afghans,
this woman, in her great unlikening,
avows it: that the body is a house.

Swayed, tinkling at some turn of thought,
like a chandelier under a dance floor,
grotesquerie so clear
there is no mistaking it for her,

she has it right: fail, be hated, die.
I have wanted to be her, saying
I am a shrine, I am a bad restaurant,
I am final under the disastrous sky.

LOCUSTS

The day the locust flew in my ear
I lay down in the circle I had mowed
and slept through sunset. Seventeen years
all my dream out in the wind
was their whisper *ignition ignition.*
How can I tell, now, pressing a finger
to lip, frost, combustible rose,
what will burn or flourish,
when they rise, shattering the streets, and sing
in the heatwave all *delay delay,*
the shrill, unbearable, of listening?

MY MISTAKE

It seems I misspoke, once, an entire roof,
shaded or lit, and unevenly littered
according to the sweep of a slender-needled pine,
and moored by one black wire to a clump of woods
and thence to everything else. I thought it was mine,
and remembered a torrent of birds there
in a morning so early it could have been the first.
But maybe it was the window, heavily in sway,
out of your parents', out of your sisters' way,
you had told me of that I was looking through.
Way up, you could make out a future
in which you would tell someone, as now I realize
you tried to, how the sun fed in the shingles,
all day, that near and nearer beast of heat
you slept against, breathless, all your last summer.
Until you packed softly, as if for one night,
and were gone forever. It amazes me.
But I who decide nothing am too often amazed,
and I should have known that window,
so vividly half sky, half slate,
was yours: since all I have left are these paler things
no one else calls love. Pardon, my mistake.

CAT AMONG STONES

Little more, but that paths contrive
dangerously to slide and how,
with softness of tread, it can draw their urge
through the lash-thin channel of its spine
in a counterflick of the tail, dissipating,
it knows. In a field, erratic in deliberation,
it tends along an isotherm,
or skirts, exactly, the lake of an odor,
as if openness itself were tortuous,
desire impassable. If it stepped across your back
you would deepen, limbless as a pond,
and go dark, all your thought
a match flame at the end of a hall,
wavering, stretched, righting itself.

POST-ROMANTIC

Now that it's over
between me and Nature
I like her better.
We've given up
senseless fear,
useless hope.
She's got herself together.

Just hanging on, but trim,
surprising, capable,
she shows, toward evening,
some of the old flashes.
If her solitudes,
amazed and kind,
can't be mine,
or her gaze of waters
stirs others,
no harm done.
She's on her own.

And don't misunderstand:
it's not yearning,
but the old courtesy
of life for life,
when sometimes, often,
out for nothing,
I stop for a minute
to hear our songs
high up, crossing.

A PAUSE

That little brown bird visiting
one corner of the meadow, then another,
for a wrapper, a twig, some fuzz-color,
is unerring, it seems, though maybe,
the world so large, so much of it dangling,
any looping out and returning
tightens, by nature, into a nest.
What is it about wonder,
strong weakness, will to be surprised,
that where there is no home, lets us live,
and just when we forget how, flies?

A MEASURE

Now that my hands are full, the world, anyway, on the fly,
and there is not time enough even to know what I know,
I take the heft of things by eye.
How many stones to that willow, how much lightning in the jay,
the drag of the jay's blue shadow across the lawn,
strict at noon, but something else at evening,
something over us like a second evening,
I can tell without stopping to lift.
I can tell from the taut soft inward of your arm
which of your fingers, driving, rests straight on the shift,
or which, consensual, is last to uncurl.
I weigh, at a distance, all of our comings together
in the story told, or lighter, untold,
on the one hand, as they say, or on the other.

OUT OF SCHOOL

In our narrow strip of wild, at any season,
though early spring, when you've begun to notice
the hard-leafed grasses and low myrtles
that have been green all winter, is when they're likely:
two girls on horses, with so much bobbing and digression
around what wind has downed or rain deepened
that you have to slow, yourself, to be sure of their heading.
It's a first love, I'm told, something like boys with dogs,
shier, though, more determined—with so strong a privacy
I can hardly show, meeting them, such broad friendliness
as between strangers on a March path,
and far from town, is endurable.
If it's sexual, as they say, how huge the obliquity.
Those outsize eyes. I can't tell: crazed, kind?
The dark, deadbolted mountain of a body.
Does a man look that way? I suppose I do,
and yet in a tale or dream, the breathing house
everyone else walks into, but that you, weakly at the door,
thunderous, soundless, fail at entering
would be your own body, wouldn't it, that, the next morning,
hopeful, or mildly resigned, and half-forgetful,
you might feed, cluck softly to, take for a jog?
Your riding on unutterable—something—
between seasons, on no path at all, near dawn,
with a friend who may or may not stay a friend?
It is the thing to do forever, I want to tell them,
meaning *I have learned nothing all these years, nothing.*
Which is true for an instant as I stumble
through the sudden give (snow yielding) of a white door
into a morning dense, like a house shut up for winter,
with leaf odor not yet coalesced as leaves:
into my life again, inviolate, unwished for.
But *nothing* is something. I could tell them—

since they think it's revelations they are waiting for—
how many of them time never will reveal.
If we diverge, with only a nod, towards what is coming,
only my silence meaning, if it can,
the world is as much yours now as it ever will be,
well, no one young could believe it—
though with our distance widened to a shout,
wavering again, I wouldn't mind stopping to hear
any voice, even my own, whisper that spring
is again unthinkable, again mysteriously clear.

EARLY VIOLETS

Because they were the first of the year,
we stopped to give what was due
to their concentration of violet
from humus and vast air.

Desire that pure could wither you,
rage strike you to your knees.
In our first year we stepped among them
unshaken, our eyes that blue.

MARIGOLDS

When you fell silent again, subsiding in your chair,
I'd tell that watchman behind your eyes our story:
how you instructed me in love of a garden,
and how, though landless in an apartment,
I scatter in harsh soil near the foundation
and on the bank that floods flash clean
our illicit and unstoppable marigolds
that flourish forgotten, hardly minding
if a dog or volley of children flattens them.
You might peer broadly, hearing that,
as into a dark room from somewhere brighter,
and begin again: *You used to follow me*
with your little wheelbarrow. But the petunias . . .
I don't remember the petunias. . . .
Where did they wilder you, those sentences
you never found the end of, trailing off,
till I rose, unnoticed? When death knocked,
Grandfather, surely you were out walking
after a word, a blossom, and out of earshot.
I would not be startled, any evening,
to see you nodding slowly at the window
like a hoer, or a great sunflower.
You might have come off a cold trail, dazed.
You might have brought from a wet, head-high meadow
rushes and loosestrife sheaved
with petunias, say, or marigolds,
a few, like large, first drops of rain,
astray on your shoulders and hair,
having blundered, sheepishly, back to a life
you could not remember ever having left.

AT FIRST, AT LAST

In this later season I find it good:
whatever cooled, and crazed in cooling.
Brightness of fracturing rivers.
That street, who would have thought it had a name?
That speech, in ruins, that we thought we understood.

There are strangers, now, where there was no one,
poignant and small.
Even the body, white frond,
is lunar and translucent, cool.

I could stop anyone in the street, invincible,
my failure a perfect disguise,
to invoke, as their myth would, the first fire
no memory touches, that would bear no eye,
though they walk on it, breathe it, think it imaginable.

*

In that country, the guest was welcomed heartily
who might be a god, and most heartily
in the green underwater light before a storm
when skirts crackle, lifting, and the yard dog mutters.
It is said: steady, meeting those sea-gray eyes,
lest they become the sea. And how, seated at their table,
strangers, also to each other, could we look away
though apples blued above us in the evening,
though we found ourselves in the open,
our hands bark, and fragrant
in the first coaxing of the rain?

*

As any antic in pajamas
and a helmet thinks he is doing,
locked in terrible argument with a city
as large as this one, touching it nowhere.

*

Hunger so pale it cannot be appeased,
they are clasped asleep in heartwood, or on the brink
of waking, forever, in inaudible thunder,
their heads stone. So the stories go,
of reward, of warning.

As if their day had slowed,
and slowing, they fell
as the drowsy sinking in of rain,
their eyes relinquished

into the wall of a lily, gaze in the round,
its bell. *To see* was at last *to hold*.
To hold within: the closing of an eye.
To die—
another intimacy we could not endure.

*

No, it is we who are the dead
and fallen, though we think we would remember
our life as the air: to be flown through, to be sung into.
When we were each other, and did not need to rage

against the where of words, and all rage spent,
murmur silly pale elegies

for love, like the blind child at the bus stop, face upturned
for the warmth, just for the warmth.

*

Had initial conditions varied
by as little as one percent
no stars would have formed,
or the stars would have stormed out
light hot elements, no carbon,
no one to sing *On and on.*

A quantum fluctuation
in the first nanosecond,
your bronze home would require
no augury, your door
open on the sun's core.

If critical constants had altered
by your early consent, unaware,
granitic shores would evaporate
at sunrise and the lake,
one level blue
cirrus, drift from its bed.

A billion universes
too hostile for us;
this one is as it is—
Anthropic Principle—
because we survive to observe it.
Who can imagine a change small enough
to make love possible?

*

That they throve with the simplicity of fiction,
those ancients, is their mystery.
That desire struck one head on,
so he took to his bed, that it departed
as in the garden dawn
departs from a stone. That he could say,
unjudged, unjudging, in the end,
as if no life were his to be taken,
having had beauty is what I have.

Now he is dead, let those others grieve.
Bring, in particular, her who, when he drank,
felt his underlip spread on the cup,
and knew the few mouthfuls, rolled around,
that coated his entire inner surface.

Because she will not be thinking of herself dead.
Nor will she attempt consolation,
since desire is inconsolable
and humble, seeing nothing of itself.
Whereas to praise wisdom is to seem wise.

*

And isn't it love, too, that wish,
each generation's, to be beyond love.

And if it fails, no one can change.
Pain builds nothing. Love is: just to be loved.

What's a story, anyway, but desire beguiled?
I'm not a kid. I don't expect to be satisfied.

Yet once I braked, downshifted, and we bowed
an instant in the same direction.

Yet once you hauled yourself from the water
and, still flowing, touched my shoulder.

*

Never for me, archaic elegy.
Passion dispelling
passionate disappearance
is our way:
of memory.

Because of my restlessness, I understand nothing.

I understand:
comfort as illusion
illusion as temporary
temporariness as permanent
permanence as comfort.

I choose my opposite for praise: patience.

If you fire a rifle straight up, at the apex,
all violence returned to potential,
you could catch the bullet between your lips.
I think of the other bullet resting
an instant on his unbruised brow.

As if to be patient were to lose nothing.

*

Someone you took for sunset is out burning,
letters maybe, in the carless lot.
Gestures large, already memory,
he stirs brief flares from a wire basket.
All he believed in will be gone

except belief, the aroma sour rose, rose horizon.
And the twilight warms with it, turning to you
with the confession, too soon,
I am much, I am so much like you.
Autumn, evening, inhalation of ghosts:
these are the lines everyone weeps over.
What a relief, our fraudulence. How real it is!
Someone has taken weariness for renunciation,
there, out late with a fire, looking for darkness.
Someone, anyone, the leaves over your shoes
in rivers, irreparable blossom.

*

In the wintry twilight, rounding a corner,
you are already too close when you see them,
one harder, one softer,
though you can't tell, really, which is the victim.
All is, experience counsels, *for the best,*
but the watering of your eyes is automatic
as if something else assumed all separation tragic.

Well, they are young excuses—them or you?
This is a school that is never out of session
whether or not you have anything to lose,
and is endured, at any age, innocently and alone,
joy and shame and heartbreak, concluding nothing,
since you can't tell, since you may never know,
whether love or freedom is the lesson.

*

If they were like me, having made all things
deathly beautiful, they left,
needing all time alone
to forgive themselves what they had done.

They are like you, taking my delighted
bending over our child as praise:
she is your child.

But if I am bitter at our life,
you are contemptuous,
having borne greater wrongs secretly,
since divine bitterness, solvent of planets,
would be fatal, even to the god.

*

On satellite infrared, false-color,
it might appear as violet, the disturbance
spreading north . . .
They are the swerveless, the slow-feeling
currents and ranges,
their vengeance, beautiful and exact,
suffering dispersion
over a whole coast, in the twelfth generation.
I feel it as spring, their accidental
exaltation or blame,
or as justice, I
who can deserve anything.

*

I have sworn never to say again
how the round-leafed plant the window dazzles
into seven huge greens
fills me with stupid happiness.
Because to dally without you
in all that precious trash of the moment
is to toy with death, or a weak
dream of it that I can bear, and worse,
to dangle before you as a grace

mere circumstance, when everywhere
lives are eaten out with famished watching.
What should I fill your eyes with but that gaze,
ungrasping, panoramic,
with which the shoals of dead face the night
for, as we are told, our power to the good
needs us poor, needs us light and free.

Or maybe not, or maybe because
I am weak and forget, or arrogant:
one more time
the songs dusting us from the fast cars all summer,
those old new songs,
sing me. *No one has said, has ever seen,
no one has ever loved like this*
go the songs of innocence. And I believe.

*

And if it is a faith you can afford,
allow me, for my services, this one word *lilac,*
and agree to know exactly what I mean

by standing eye-deep in its odor, by the cringe
from groin to panged tongue,
as if some shame you can't remember struggled out
the same door in every cell
impossible beauty was trying to get in.

As if the sea were lilacs,
combers of them, rustling cones.
Sootheless now as spring, their animal restlessness.
Almost passion, their rush among the pilings.

*

Their terrible austerity quaint now,
the silence at their tombs, melodramatic,
alas, alas, the gods are strictly poetic.
And who can revere their slangy progeny
in Deco temples of the Thirties
like unto refrigerators,
or glass-curtained Manhattan,
less awful than my stereo, my laptop?
I hear of brilliant heartlessness
and sex as uninflected and free
as the black-lined glint of vapor lamps
at midnight on the continental parking lot.
I think I already know how to desire
its gods, their vertical pupils, silver hair,
and the night they deal, so ravishing and corrosive
even the skyline will not return.
But I know what will happen to them,
alas, and I cannot worship anymore
because the gods, the gods have grown too young.

*

How fragile, Sunday on the avenue,
as if some desperation had been removed, some protection.
All the couples just up are carrying bakery bags
slowly, elbows in, hearing out wide.
And the amazed geezers piloting their cars,
larger somehow, windblown.

*

And when the rains had hardly slackened
fires broke out, and everywhere on the hills
your gaze lit, yes, the blur of heat,
and a cardinal of flame, alarm.

In the global warming: your hair pulled tight,
kerchiefed, unclean,
your lips dark and slick, your blouse
translucent, sinking in *Can you want this?*
No one can lift this.

In the fever *Can you want this?*
the street, in suffering twilight, pooled
in our black drive, the dandelions
gone to frail puff, lifting
in a long tongue through the chainlink, tin-tinning.

And to be free, you decided you would never sleep,
and the second night *Can you want this?*
the light staying on in your brain
showed you busy, quiet reefs,
bruise-like anemones, gingerly currents

of the ocean in the fever
rising, feeling our rooms.
And you woke to look,
and found no difference waking,
no mystery, nothing clear,
desire nothing held
and a match hiss *yes.*

*

This too shall pass they say
you can say anyway.

And yet the opposite is also true
will often do.

What goes up vanishes.
Things fall of their own weightlessness.

Therefore we bless our errors,
true to us forever.

Who loves his disease,
to be cured must be cured of love.

Yet even to say *I believe nothing*
how much you have to believe.

*

The ingenuity of our kindness, first,
the heat of the pillows,
and the reminder I left folded on your desk
will become unreadable.
O, as early as tomorrow,
all memory overwritten
of the forty years it took us to get here,
and only half-here—bitter, relieved, regretful
—they will say a single wave, transcontinental,
dropped us walking distance from where we are,
the site of the house uncertain; our burial, simple,
without household implements, and far from water.

*

And why, since even the air
buries them, or the eye's transparency,
and they can touch nothing as themselves,
but, grotesque in need, bear on us
as swan, canyon, runnel of gold—
why should they not be given in compensation
silly powers: stone-breaking glances, the choosing of winds?
They who, knowing to the end, can wish for nothing,
would wish if they could
that we did not think we believed in them,

or that we could not, in our ignorance, compose
stories so like their knowledge, weightless:
Once upon a time. The end.

*

Fame I could wait for.
Money I worried about but did not love.
Love I had and hadn't
according, I thought, to my will.
Which was the god, then,
I honored with obsession,
until, worn smooth
and joyless by the repetition,
I remember nothing
except again and again
trying to write out, just once, his name?

And when from its weakness
or my strength
language disobeys,
and every word
two sentences
speaks or speak,
and I can say nothing,
I come again,
tireder now, wanting nothing,
to a place I can hear,
as I heard when younger,
next year next year?

*

Never, or in another country, the ending:
whoever would have been its author,
a mere character by then, and ignorant,

remembers *They were in another story*
and our patience with beginnings,
as it must, begins.

*

I am younger than my friends
and their children
and their children's children
I wrote and unwrote when I was twenty,
not sure what it meant.
Thought I can neither enter nor forget,
a room you might be sleeping in.

AS IF ENDING

Because Kate stood, face pushed to the screen,
cheering *fuck off, fuck off*
into the swim of summer,
I don't know what, but *because*
opening day-wide into the milling of crows,
and what will come later, their comical rage . . .

Even, today, the tactfulness of death,
how it delays so long we can believe anything:
we are dead already, we are immortal,
that the sight of our child, or only
all this guessing brings it on.

Everywhere, this season, I remember
a couple at a railing, leaning out.
What they are saying I can never hear, but it means
it is impossible to stay together,
and since that changes everything, they stay.

How can they be us—they have only just met,
remember nothing, do not know what they are doing,
think, wonderingly, of their lives
grace not ours, violence not ours.
As if they too had been there yesterday,
when a migration little different from evening,
leveling, took its long place on the water,
ending nothing, since nothing ends.

HOW THINGS ARE (2000)

HOW THINGS ARE: A SUITE FOR LUCRETIANS

The new molecular philosophy shows astronomical
interspaces betwixt atom and atom, shows that the
world is all outside; it has no inside.

        —Emerson

1

Because the oysters I sucked down
were swished with Red Tide,
the fleeing of the stars
shifts red tonight.

Running a red
with the radio loud
or singing under a green,
even my brain's less mine—

Ah, Long Island wine,
and my new taste in ties!
Like you, I've seen what no one else has seen.
The universe will die before I die.

2

So it is spring, the season, as Lucretius says,
of Desire, skill of the world. Alas, so hurtfully young,
rumple of sheets still faintly on her cheeks,
she wanders, flushed, one button half out,
like a tongue just touching the back of the teeth,
or tangles on the floodplain's picnic blankets
in tableaus the iconographer would call

Venus enveloping hardbody Mars,
sleepily appeased, Love sapping War.

I like the other allegories better:
ice binding fire; or form and matter;
or sympathy and . . . whatever keeps us at our ourselves
when we are licked at, lapped at by desire.
The sand is swept downstream in toughening waters,
the breeze grows keen with smoke, the evening dense
with lovers its half-closed eyes have blurred together.
Listen up. And I will disclose to you the laws of heaven.

3

If there were no such thing as empty space, Lucretius says,
no atom could move, no new thought enter this universe:
there is no fecundity without emptiness.
Yet nothing can come of nothing without seed or cause.
Otherwise bluebirds, shaking off dust,
would hatch from the harrowed fields, and cattle,
lowing, amble from the storm-green sky.
All things randomly would greet and deny us, feed and fail us,
and creatures would flood rockwaste and woods indifferently,
gnashing at leaf and stone and nothing at all,
mistaking hunger for their food, and for their joy, austerity
                    and pain,
but none of this can be imagined.

Men would stride out of the river, memoryless.
They would imagine themselves immortal,
and ride the trains bird-eyed, imploring, homicidal.
They might mistake love for a deadly thing
and batter children to save themselves from pity,
or shoot from a rooftop a crone swaying behind a laundry cart
as you might practice your deadly topspin serve.
But none of this can be imagined.

4

Between the Millstone River, just downstream
from the Sewer Authority,
and the Delaware and Raritan Canal
(disused) which two warm days
turn much too green

is a towpath, where you might surprise
a tangle of bikes
or a carp some laid-off fisherman, aghast
at its sheer albino size

has left to a mannerly crow
that lifts, as from gift wrap,
quivering scarves,
rose-dust, and smoky blue, and mauve,

or the pink-eyed
guy with skinzines,

or me with my roar of a walk
and Walkman, head wide
with ten-in-a-chain moon-glossy
(oops I've been singing)
junk mail songs

O reader, dear!
(You have already won)
Never, O never before
(Our sympathy . . .)

Water, water, everywhere . . .
Though it probably wouldn't kill me.

5

For if each thing did not have its essence and seed
nothing would prevent a single tree from bearing
all fruits ridiculously, or each in its season,
and the mind would be lost in every image crossing it.
Parents would shudder and revert to infancy,
old men, mouths softening, turn into women.
Just by closing your eyes, you could distinguish the planets
by taste (those rocky herbs, red and green and blue),
or six pistons superheated, or each friend's failure,
but none of this can be imagined.

You would thrill with the narrow wind of the beast's desire,
glass wind of the stone's.
You would know how the deer's mind, leaping,
tones like the air in a flute, silver
and sudden as the long lake glimpsed through trees.
You would know through desire how to become anything,
as the lake holds any cloud, each sad migration,
each wooden bottom, each suddenly outcast line
it seems to itself to conceive of.

6

Because my immunity was compromised
I was invaded by living particles,
because I stepped ankle-deep through the ice
I was cirrus, keen across the moon,

because of stress,
because I scorned two aspirin and bed rest,
resigned myself to the poverty of pure relation,
neglected my office, hardly propitiated

Fever, the rock-bound Titan,
or *because,*

I have every disease.
I have heart shutting down.
I have noon, my brow hot lily.
I have evening's
repeating crickets, metastatic.
I have the bull's-eye rashness.
I have the undone.
I have August, terminally.
I have sleeping on an open magazine.
I have white, chronic dawns.

7

Nothing we know, Lucretius says, is nothing:
the unseen wind, he reminds us, must be bodies
small and soft enough to stir single hairs on your wrist
or find places on your skin so secret and grateful
you cannot tell the feeling of them from your feelings.
Yet surely they have hardness and strength in concert,
since they can herd a bank of clouds sky-long without
                    derangement,
erect from the sea eighty-foot walls, or slide a ship
with the flat patience of continental drift,
just as rivers whisk houses from their foundations,
or wear canyons so slowly it hurts to think of the slowness,
even though water seems the softest thing to us
because we are water, and touch ourselves, touching it.

Similarly, downwind of a burning house,
you smell the fire-tang and your eyes water
though you saw no odors approaching, their ambush
so sudden, so much like remembering,

you have to remind yourself they are not everywhere.
No, they're a lake you can wade into, or walk out of:
as in the car I hold myself in the wind,
with your swift, O too swift, silence next to me,
and smell lilac for a mile, then henhouse,
diesel, mildew, laundry and what else,
as if a book went by too fast to understand,
or a runner's ripe heat, running just behind her.

8

Nothing is easier than that you assume me,
though if I squeezed next to you on the bus, smelling of wool
                                    and rain,
we might smile tightly and never look to the side.

You would not want to overhear my bitter prayer,
my thought of your perfume, least of all your name.
Like you I walked with my family and was helpless love.
Like you I wished for their destruction, not knowing I was
                                    wishing.
Like you I was granted perfections and did not feel them
                                    undeserved.
Like you I dreamed of making love to myself,
wondered if anyone saw exactly the blue I see,
knew no one was moved as I was by that love that song that
                                    season
and no one was bored as I was by that love, song, season,
knew you as myself, and did not know myself.

This entire warm front was breathed last week in Omaha,
rebreathed in Cleveland, and already
see how these long sentences lie down in you, knowing,
is it, or already known? You cannot stop hearing them,
though I am modest, I am polite. How is it possible

to be alone, since someone is always speaking
in the head, someone is always reading,
with a chancy candle, the middle of a sentence
that begins and ends in darkness.
                              Here, I am long gone
from behind these words, yet you hear them talking,
as the gull's cry seems to be coming from far behind the gull.

9

Nothing is just *out there,* Lucretius says;
its particles must enter us to be known.
Smell, for example, is the lounging of inhalations
along receptors complementary in form,
like fingers spreading for a difficult chord,
or the whole sky sliding soundlessly to dock
in the fine-toothed harbors of a fern.

That softly-repeated *plinking* on a jar,
distant at first? Listen more closely:
the rain's tower rises, and you walk,
steps echoing, in a huge cathedral
of hearing that has somehow entered you.
Hills left carelessly under the horizon
like someone sleeping, the sky, cloud-sifted sun
settle like fine gauze on our open faces
as if we were daisies, blind in the fall of pollen.

As for your slow extrusion from the ocean
failing colorlessly down your sides,
lift of your thighs against reluctance:
I *feel* it, I say, as if the eyes were hands,
for it is true, as desire tells us, that the world is touch,
or being touched—no telling the difference.
Always the shifting of tumblers, the whisper *Open,*

just as, moving against you at dawn, and lightly,
I am gray windows slowly lightening.

10

I can't get it through my head that the day is just in my head:
that I don't see *things,* only reflected light.
That I don't see light, actually, flitting between perches,
just the splash on my retina, the ripple
inward, of chemical potentials,
which isn't seeing at all—I mean, as I think of it.

It's as if I were watching behind video goggles
a movie of exactly the path I'm taking,
hearing on tape exactly what I hear,
though to God, looking down in trans-sensual knowledge,
it's darkness and silence we walk in,
the brightness and noise only in our heads,
which are the few lit windows in a darkened office tower.

11

But Lucretius, who does not believe in light,
not really, says that we see because things broadcast
images of themselves, continuous, that are material.
That jogger is shedding skins of herself like frames of a film
entering my eyes. The revolutions of the moon send down
husks of a moon, tree calls endless *treeeee* into the wind.
So the moon is itself a wind, the tree is a wind of seeing,
and the rose throws *rose* and *rose* down your welling eyes.

Naturally, the air is crowded with these films.
Your image, for example, and a wayward *horse*
superimposing, *centaur* might come to mind, though faintly

since such a thing never was. Imagination, we call it,
or dream, because these simulacra are so fine
they can enter through the skin, asleep, or any opening.
So, too, when *rose* and *moon* and *jogger* blend like winds:
I feel running in the skies, and a thorn of breath,
a gust of sweat and roses passing,
a body of moon my hands of moon pass through.

Images of all that has ever happened, further,
and all who have ever been, alive or dead,
persist in every place, at any time.
I concentrate, and your paleness rises through the throng
of clamoring shades. I.e., I remember you.
For the air itself is memory, everything's stored there:
faces we seek and recognize, all those strangers
who populate our dreams, or rise to become the faces
in books we read. It is all the air on our faces.

This is why no one asks you for your secrets.
Your whispers of love and shame in apparent privacy
are already heard, but so faintly who can be sure
whether it's you, imagination or the air,
in this life or the last, that whispers in them?
Now, as my past grows longer, things I did
in my faint youth are fainter than someone else's,
and things I have dreamed of, over and over,
stories I've read, lives scented on the wind
or distantly adored, history, imagination,
are strong as what was mine. I call them true. I call them truer.

12

The sun is bright because its images dive steeply
into our eyes, ninety million miles.
The breeze they drive before them

is how distance, Lucretius says,

is sensed in the eyes. Can you feel this
when you open to my gaze:
how the eyes themselves are wind,
wind with a question's rising intonation?

13

This is how it goes: all you are saying
expands in a sphere, an organized explosion,
though blurring, with distance, into wordless intonation,
until its vagueness, at last encompassing everything,
becomes unhearable motions, displacement of a pane,
rocking of airborne particles, faint heat in the walls
that not even a god's hearing can turn back into words.
Nor can you take them back, no more than remove
the blush from a cheek, these your root
in the world, your touch of everything again.

There is no standing that is not sending everywhere,
no waiting that does not rush out at lightspeed.
Even the un-happened, the never-told,
for these gave form to all you did, are raying out
to shape the future, though impossible, though unheard,
as my call ringing and ringing in your room,
and ceasing, leaves the silence ringing.

14

Dust of singer on singer, bird on bird,
dust of their images, broadcast,
dust of their songs that settles
on monitors and end tables

and in me, residuals of wind,
so I must be seen again, to grow light
after much fatness of seeing,
must speak, not to drown in hearing.

15

If everything is touch, then what's this soft
devouring of your drifts and drives, this blowing
through your tops and outlooks, under your shuddering doors,
this smoothing you like a map, or folding you small
to fit you into all these stories
I have to tell, this feeling you fit me into yours.
this saying O you *this?*

If I am the trillion fingertips of air
you form beneath, if we are waters blended,
perfumes unstoppered, gone and everywhere,
have I reached you, do I grasp you?
If I stand in you, my eyes behind your eyes,
if I underlie your breathing, rising where you rise
and cleaving where you cleave? Is it knowing

at all, this saying
that tries to be like seeing, this seeing trying to be heard,
these sentences, which are one further sense,
straining to vanish into something they call you,
or to be vanished *into,* as a lake makes
so much of its forgetting of the rain?

16

And if, as I dream, I touched you microscopically
as smoke touches air, if I entered you

at the level of the molecule, your carbon chains
stretching like power lines into a starless sky,

it would be dark, for there are no eyes on this scale,
and there's nothing to see, anyway, no face of yours
in no beneficent sky, no windy soul,
no signatory flourish of your limbs,
just atoms, like invisible constellations,
and light waves, propagating past me darkly,
as if I stood blind and deaf, even my thoughts turned off,
on the shaken platform of the Express.

This inside I've imagined would be an outside,
this merger I've desired, a further distance,
lucid, stellar, cold. O you *you*
who are a galaxy that has never heard of you,
as words have never heard of a beautiful line
or the beautiful line of its explanation.

17

Thus for our lightly, fluently repeated
wish to be light or wind or water—to be pure *move*
and blend as movements—wind and light and wind—
and no more rage at our massiveness and boredom,
that not-wanting-to-be-loved
undoing all our dreams of who we were,
wind in light and cloud in light in wind.

But then: the pillar taller than my body, the slammed door,
the light on the sill, the cliff between two notes,
the shelf booked-up in size-order, even the oft-sung pear
that reminds us, as everything else does, of the body,
and yes, even its truly boring
and sad oft-sungness,

and a tire's hot squeal, letting go,
are desire, and difficult, and difficult desire.
Why should I not have a garage,
a swabbed counter, a geode,
why should I not have a dog for a heart?

18

Why touch me, anyway, if *nearness* is just a metaphor
that leaves us in the cold? But to feel what planets feel,
holding each other to their swift ellipses,
their swinging out a form of their falling in: speak

around me, then, let me misunderstand
deeply, fail to compare yourself to me,
smiling stubbornly. Rise so steeply
I can clamber up, scatter my equipment,
sleep, and wake to mountains of the dawn.

19

For we have never, strangely, been within ourselves.
Never have I sailed the red arterial grotto
to my thick hand, have never and never
seen the mauve noon there, like the sun through squeezed lids.
I imagine the air mid-palm as dense and tropical,
but there is no air; breathing there is sub-marine,
continuous but hidden, molecular like time,
and, like time, runs without our willing

as even our will does. I say *I will walk*, but given the power
over walking, I would fall debating which nerves to fire,
which of a score of muscles to contract in order.
If I were responsible for everything in my body,

I would pass out from mismanagement of glands
I don't even know the names of. As for the legions
of mitochondria and ion channels, how would I supervise them,
and still remember to draw breath in, to beat my heart,
as if I were charged with counting *a million, a million and one*
in a million voices simultaneously?

The body is what is done for us. From it
our dream of the world's beneficence derives,
from it, too, our helplessness, since, floating above it,
we do not know what we do or how we do it.
Thus our intensest pleasures, alone or together,
are pleasures, too, because they lose us in our bodies
with a slow perfection. I taste and fail,

or let music sway me with the wide slowness
of a plucked string in strobe. *It is rich to die,* I say,
torrents of darkness filling my closed eyes.
Old metaphor, but true, since it is true in dying,
whether from gunshot, heart attack, or cancer,
the last thing is: cells starve for oxygen and go down.
All deaths, in the end, are drownings in the body,
as what desire desires is drowning in desire.

20

Pretty convincing, what the brain's
original darkness, guessing what light was like,
came up with: eye.
As for the ear?
Ah, what it thought of air.

This plane in turbulence, dropping abruptly,
this one-more-stair-than-I-thought,
my foot sunk in the mole-soft lawn,

the wounded falling towards their wounds,
these swallows, hitting the sunset, gone,

must be what I've made of you: November,
white-blue and high
chamber in the catacomb
desire has hollowed, prisoner for life.

21

Come the thunderbolts, such is their suddenness
who knows whether they made us afraid, or our fear
or guilt summoned them, wrath of Zeus?
Thus when we hear what we least wanted to hear,
which means, of course, that we expected it somehow,
we say *It hit me like a thunderbolt.*

For the mind is not a point, as we sometimes think,
or the little theater where we sit alone, but many nations,
eye, ear, memory, knowing, knowing of knowing,
each in contact with the others by Long Distance,
and there's no one Place that is us, no single Present,
only the order in which we hear their calls.

So much that happens to us is ourselves, is timing.
A man who seemed to *think* of lightning, birds, a face
a millisecond before he knew he had *seen* them
might feel he was a god and had called them down,
or, take the milder case, might grow up feeling his power
because so much took place as he foresaw, or milder still,
might feel the world as a friendliness of happening.

Whereas the one who heard himself speaking words
a millisecond before he knew he'd chosen to say them
would find them like lightning. Would think

Even my own words happen to me.
I lie here, dead, listening for the voice of the god,
though even my listening is His Will in me,
as on the tip of a downbent branch, a dampish sparrow
opens its throat to admit a cry.

22

Hawks, rockets, lightning are fast, but the mind
concludes these journeys almost before they are thought of.
To Sirius? A matter of milliseconds. Ah, but how
do the continents remember to keep drifting
at a rate that imperceptibly becomes an inch a year,
how does the frost with a week's pressure,
such delicate and terrific pressure from every side at once,
harden and brown a weed without breaking a single stamen,
or in fifty years turn a hair gray? Slow's the wonder.

So many phenomena it pleases us to think of
as beyond process or performance, help or hindrance—
the reassertion over scarred ground, for example,
of the weeds, or the congregation of the clouds—
because to think of them this way (which means not
to think of them) leaves something in us free
and the world wild and full of gifts, what we call *real*.
Slow's the wonder; slow's the relief. But even wonders
have their essences and seeds, and patiently grow from them,

for time also is particulate, as Lucretius tells us, atom by atom.
Thus your wedding ring, over decades, slims with wear,
and a plowblade down the sillion shines and dwindles
as a knife with sharpening silvers into the air.
Lanes blacken gradually with the passing of tires,
and the stone stair is worn in the middle as if sagging
with heavy feet, and when it rains the water courses there.

Even the legendary lightning, slowly seen,
is a man descending a ladder, stopping to look down,
starting again to descend. Even light,
scrupulously imagined, is gradual,
though when will you calm, when will you ever gaze
with the steady openness that would slow its radiation,
showing the smooth striving from streetlamp down to street
of the individual waves, over and over?

Ah, everything happens for cause, and gradually,
and nothing disappears at once, or totally:
this is the thing Lucretius seems to tells us
that we most wanted to be told. That time
is also touch, and can be touched again,
and always the *having been* leaves traces of its being,
as if it remembered and would never leave us alone.

Or that's what we believe, regardless, we who trek
to the stairs the poet's foot wore, or look out the windows,
strangely askew now, of our childhood homes,
or weep for pleasure in apartments of old pain,
or greet the traveler who once stopped to listen
to crickets in the field, where, rumor has it,
the lover of the goddess rained down, blasted,
though reason insists coincidence of place is nothing.

For the mind itself is suasions of erosion
if we could pay attention—but that is the point,
isn't it? No one notices, in all the backing and forthing,
how the beach re-contours. "Suddenly," it is changed,
something is gone you thought was a love forever,
something lifted you thought would be heavy forever.
In the novel the children grow up in a sentence
and a young man wakes up gray and over, and Lucretius
. . . but now— gods, make me slower!— I cannot remember
how it took forty-odd years to get here,

page whatever, a matter of inches from the beginning.
And if I can't re-live it, second by second,
feeling the constant assurance of faint time
like the slight burn of kite string paying out through two fingers—
as, alas, who can?—then it is not mine,
and there is no such thing as a life, and my next step
may thrust into blankness white as the end of a line

23

Though Zeno, with his arrow that must travel
half the distance to your heart, then half of what remains,
and half of that, and never arrives,
proves motion impossible, since how could the arrow
                              remember
over the huge chasm between instants
that it should be moving? So I am always half-way
to half-way to understanding: that the present does not exist,
though once it must have, since . . . see
all I cannot move back to!

Or maybe it's that we do not live in the present,
which is the rock in the stream
that splits us as we flow around it.

24

And I'm still not sure everything isn't fire
        as Heraclitus says,
sunfire starfire steelfire,
        or, slow-thirsting, burning coolly,
rockfire lakefire;
        since all our senses perceive,
rosefire jayfire,

since chestfire, all I feel, and eyefire,
since the mind, too,
            like the fire in the hearth, its faces,
fire and darkfire forming each other,
            since the mind,
like all things in the windfire
            tears and shifts,
since
            timefire

25

But all things have an essence, and a time, and take their time.
Otherwise, why could not Nature produce men of such power
they could traverse the ocean as if it were nothing more
than blue carpet, dampish on a humid morning,
and break off Andes like the heel of a loaf?
They might eat the planet clean, or replant it
with aluminum forest and weep at its ruin.
They might, in whimsy, channelize our Southern rivers,
leaving them straight and navigable—
what could be simpler or clearer?—
and if they were also scoured of life, silt-choked, flood-prone . . .
well, here is the law of the universe, first,
that everything we imagine is too simple for us,
and second that our desires, given their way,
are powerless to undo their own undoings.
For desire simplifies and forgets, and Lucretius reminds us
things are more easily taken apart than put back together.
How could we live in a world that abided our consent?
I think of you turned to mine, to me, to yours,
to someone else's, to what you wanted.
I think, don't you, of our grade school art class—
how we waited in line to pour in the sink our rinsings,
how all of our visions, finally mixed,

made, every week, the same brown disappointed waters?

26

For all things are made also of what resists them.
Otherwise each Atlantic wave, incoming,
might spread over the prairies like a sky, and never stopping,
meet the Pacific, or each single, barely perceptible
spore of a fern might suddenly unfold
over us a green map the size of the world.

The peach, in its seed-instant, already turns and turns
as if the opposing air were coded in its dream
of how roundly it will ripen against the sky:
the essence of things is foreknowledge of their limits,
as the mime's body shapes itself backwards from finger
to shoulder with the touch of a wall it will never touch.

Thus for imagination, thus for desire:
time is the enemy they deepen against,
though it alone denies the return of the dead
they ached for, and all those loves unhappening.
It alone saves us from subjugation to freedom, it alone
prevents the fruitless practice of perfection.
Otherwise all stories are equally true
and there is no success or failure, heroism or shame,
no love some other story won't undo.
Otherwise nothing is left to the imagination,
otherwise there is no otherwise.

AFTERWORD

How Things Are: A Suite for Lucretians

Lucretius is one of those authors I can't imagine not having read, though he came along late in my virtually Latinless education, in the last course of a graduate program I happily survived by completely failing to understand what was expected of me. In the Mantinband translation of *De Rerum Natura* we used back in the 70's, he sounded like this:

> *For nothing can touch or be touched, unless it possesses body*
> *And garments hung up by the sea-washed shore grow damp,*
> *but, spread out in the sunshine, they become quite dry.*
> *Yet no one has ever seen how the water came into them,*
> *or how it went away again in the heat of the sun.*
> *Therefore water consists of tiny particles*
> *which it is impossible for our eyes to see.*

A scientist at a time when science, philosophy and poetry were not necessarily different, Lucretius explains the atomic theory of matter in language as plain and literal as possible. But how plain is that? "Plain" and "literal" are themselves metaphors, and even rationalism's most scraped-clean explanations are stories: in passages like this I found a strangely disembodied body, the secret ministries of invisible particles, an austere but heartening animation in the mere drying of beach towels. And how much stronger the sense of transparency, of Presence, when Lucretius pulled out all the stops and turned the sturdy present into a panorama of secret and lovely erosions:

> *Moreover, in the course of many revolving years,*
> *a ring on someone's finger is made thin by wear,*
> *and dripping water hollows a stone, and an iron plowshare*
> *imperceptibly diminishes in the fields.*
> *The paving-stone of the highway is all rubbed away by human feet,*
> *and brazen statues near the gates often have the right hand partly*
> > *worn away*
> *as people pass along and touch it for a greeting.*

117

We know these things diminish, since they are rubbed away,
and yet which particles fall off, and at what times,
our jealous faculty of sight prevents us from seeing.

This landscape was the one I lived in, or needed to, and I had found something like it in the Victorians I most loved. Hardy's novels and poems are full of worn stairs, shoulder-brushed jambs, haunted places. When he traveled to Europe, he gravitated to the graves of Keats and Gibbons, the field where Shelley's skylark might have crashed. He refused invitations to America: it had no ghosts of interest to him. What he felt was what Tennyson called "the passion of [not 'for'] the past." I trust in this context I won't have to explain, as I often did to incredulous friends, why I thought "Transformations" was his best poem:

> *These grasses must be made*
> *Of her who often prayed,*
> *Last century, for repose;*
> *And the fair girl long ago*
> *Whom I often tried to know*
> *May be entering this rose. . . .*

or why these lines of Whitman

> *This grass is very dark to be from white heads of old mothers,*
> *Darker than the colorless beards of old men,*
> *Dark to come from under the faint red roofs of mouths.*

seemed to me his most moving. No, say his most *touching.* For Hardy and Whitman, though two thousand years later, live in a Lucretian community of touch. To minds both literal and superstitious enough (and what mind isn't enough of both?), time's recoverable. Those eroded particles are the trail of bread crumbs back to where we were. Everything that's gone touched something that touched something else that we can still see and touch. Isn't it all still there, then, trying to remember itself in us? That's a desperate world-size metonymy we can't quite believe, of course, skeptics and rationalists that we are. But then, of course, we can't stop believing it either.

Lucretius is a brilliant scientist and a teacher just as brilliant. I don't pretend that "How Things Are: A Suite for Lucretians" qualifies as scientific, though its reader will not be surprised to hear that I subscribe to more science magazines than literary ones, or even that it's more than tangentially Lucretian, an homage, a fantasia. As for teacherliness: I've characterized the tone to myself as "faux-didactic." There's a deadpan faintly amused at itself, a kind of lecturer who fairly often runs off the rails being over-logical or over-lyrical. I'm aware the poem makes points about metaphor, about the isolation of the mind, about imagination and the adequacy of the world thereto, but they weren't The Point. If there's an overall argument, it came late and was elicited largely by changing the order of sections written for their own sakes until their sequence made as much sense as it could. It was like doing one of those games on the old HoJo place mats: connect the dots in the right order and you've drawn a face, or spelled out d-e-s-i-r-e.

What's it like to *be*, physically? To be alone? Together? What's *In,* how's *With,* where's *To?* I suppose the need to think those basic terms over and over is what makes one what's called a "nature poet," a term I detest. When I was a young man, my story was that I'd started out wanting to be a physicist or chemist and that adolescence had diverted me into poetry. In actuality, I was always terrible in the lab. There was always some measurement I knew would be interesting that I didn't have the tools or the discipline or (over and over) the patience with reality to come up with. Now it seems to me that what I really wanted was to be something more like an alchemist, and that I kept right on.

UNDER WATER

1   The Flood

So even having heard the news, I stayed
by the bay window, page unturning,
as the water rose, as it was growing
unsuddenly out of the air, like evening,
wetless, exactly body temperature,
and with such slight adjustment, breathable,
that only my slowing hands showed it was there.

Like your *Listen!* as it branches up a stairwell,
or your voice at a question's end, it rose.
With a faint jangle of hangers, closets were emptied,
with a soft shuddering, the drawers,
and the walls subsiding and the lapse of doors
were an old song played back too slowly,
the *I* and *love* now moaning *youuu* and *ohhh*.

And I heard (because sound travels under water)
the dinner mutter of my neighbors,
untroubled, nothing about the water,
though there passed from left to right across my window
what must have been their furniture,
and to the glass loomed momentarily
and open-mouthed one or the other of their daughters.

Swallows, without a wingbeat, pour through evening
slowly as floaters dimly behind my gaze,
the phone rings, ember-slow, and streetlamps,
slowly as dragged-on cigarettes, grow strong.
The luster of eyes is an hour rising or draining,
and lightning of revelation, when it comes,
is a hand passing slowly down my face.

A glass of daffodils (for spring is floodtime)
at these depths is a blowless yellow gale,
the piano, in a haze of keys, faint savor.
Reach of my arms for reachlessness,
bay of my gaze now lessening in blue,
and all I have called my body: held notes failing,
as if I were being remembered, but vaguely.

2 *Little Bridge*

Suffering and smoking on the little bridge
(teen, as I remind myself, means *misery)*
they look up, glaze, the two of them,
Cancel alert: slow herbivore,
their scorn of me too lazy to be scorn,
my pity of them unfair, and not quite pity.

They could be us, in Year Whatever.
Same bridge. Same evening,
gazing into the water where your face,
as you straightened up to go,
expanded downstream,
and now is Now.
                        If it were not for time,
I could be walking, right here, through your body.
I could be you. If not for the heart,
that will not let anything be,
that will not let anything be gone.

3 Salvage

Ever since Sanitation skimmed from the Outer Harbor
that sole impala, pale
with a driftwood phosphorescence,
I have known they survive, those drowned lands.
So gradual the invasion of the ocean
that the herds could mix again with waters,
browse Sargasso, stream Gulf Stream,
till their hooves lost touch with those savannas,
and veering, they sailed

as tawny, carnal clouds over the dream
that finds me in my childhood home,
still smoking, wrongly married,
trying to read what will have been
on a page ablur with dream-water.
All night, dark whale of sky goes over,
and dully the sandy lion of the combers,
and the rivers, long birds gliding in.

4 Undersong

Because I heard, under your murmur,
river as *swerve,* and pondering
pondering, the waves;
because it would not cease,
tree the jay's cry *tree,* and in the leaves,
alluvial, the rain's plural;
because it goes on and on,
though going, gone, our whither-thou-
ghost of a chance . . .

Say *leaves, leaving,* blending *lull* and *weave,*
as in *the leave of my hands over you.*

How they float intently and slowly
like a prayer in no direction
fill   leave   save   fail
or repeating, repeating, trying not to forget
a very long number;
like words, so wide now and so *were*
that they will not say *no you are, no you are*

5   *Letter from One of Many Worlds*

As you knock, if it's even you, a thousand universes,
like the moths on the screen door, wildly diverge.
In most, nobody's home. In some, somebody
dawdles or hurries to the door, bemused or eager,
with thoughts like these, if he's me, if he hears.

Or else you do not knock and, turning, meet me
as a bus brakes noisily and sparrows panic
and I walk out of sunset from another story,
wide-eyed with the early dark, and with the wonder
that my arms are full of groceries, and that you know me.

And of these stories, millioning their ways,
and of the sparrows, reeling, we are every one,
and in each eye the glint of all the others.
It is said these branchings, infinite, are the god.
If so, a god so swift it cannot remember.

Which is why, fond stranger, only I could tell you
of that other life in which I love you even now,
how we slept in pine-wind in a cold arboreal land,
how the faint ache down your arm and your shy, bewildered
                    pride,
were once for a child that, now, you have never had.

But since no two of us have come by the same ways,
not even love's first lovers would dare to whisper
What do you know, what do you really remember?
and we live, as thieves stick to their alibis,
this life of which nothing is an example.

6 *River Sunset*

The brazen or sun-blonde,
the melon river, catching in its bend
faint slur of sundown, or the spray,
blood-golden, of a swallow.
The water grayed and mauve, aqua water,
whelmings and rinsings of your hair and sides
and grounds and fruit bruise and perfume,
all the taste of you swept
in a long tongue downstream,

where the deer look up,
where whoever plunged from the little bridge,
where softly on the lawn
(and sharply you remembered)
your foot sank down,
where the fabulous deluge,
and the creatures, two by two, would prove
there is nothing anyone,
not even the gods, may unimagine . . .

Under the moody clouds, under the thunder
played back too slowly to be understood,
some story you could not get out of your head
of the poor one unsolaced—
blue willows, island of Shalott,
peril of mirror or abolished tower—
who enters the long-souled

touch of the river,
where the coroner's boy,
poling the shallows,
draws up, gowned in river grass,
whom the water dissembles
whatever they were,
as beautiful lost women,
their silks untoppled, their lips
(and barely, you imagine)
wet by fastidious tides . . .

7 *Water Music*

And then she said, as if we were walking on the ocean bottom,
though it was a damp, soft-shouldered, stony road
in fog dense and free as darkness, early autumn,
our voices fog-reflected, hollowed. And then she said,
when a hundred feet off in the fog, where there was nothing,
brakelights flowered, and an engine kicked hastily in,
and a deer flickered through the rose air and was gone.
She said *he* said: something about fires dying,
growing, the road not taken, moving along,
something about self-something I'd have blushed at in a book,
though, as three rising and twining columns of smoke,
freedom and love and endurance above the ruin,
her pain, the child's, his, thinning to near-falsetto,
it could have been heartbreaking in a song.
Those were the words it gave her: what could she do but sing?
And what was my role but the unreflecting friend,
who turns, arms wide, to the darkened audience,
with *O the pity,* as it is written, and *Cruel destiny!*
and sparing no hyperbole of gesture
to say: *Forgive the badness of translation.*
This, as you know well, is tragedy.
Be grateful for the embarrassing simplicity

that allows you to stay, for two hours, just who you are.
Words fail her; they are supposed to fail,
and failing, become the intuition of the wish
she cannot see now will be too easily granted:
to be us, *who hear, still settling in our seats,*
her song O, this is nothing you have heard
and her song-to-come It was an old, old story.
Shouldn't I sing this to her, shouldn't a curtain . . .
shouldn't the moon break through now, or a cry made strange in
                the fog?
but it is art that is short, and this, this would be long,
and we had already scared off what was in the dark, and were
                alone.

8 *The Water As It Was*

Which at the velocity
of divers from the Verrazano
might as well be concrete . . .
Say here in the ancient ocean momently grown hard
these square foundations,
these doors
swaying and shutting with the ebb and surge,
these atria
failing of sill and caller,
damage and rule,
say this is the house
built of all the stones I ever threw in the water.

9 *The Dreaming-Back*

You would be surprised what stays:
the turn in the stairs
with the little table, the age in your face
that finally turned you mine.

Like the instant of drowning, some say,
or (the obliquity of the world over)
the dead's helpless remembering
according to intensity,
no way to tell memory from dream.

All things granted, now,
why should they care for desire?
The most trivial sin they could not confess,
some uncalled-for explanation
never explained away,

refusals, sheer dull presences:
these, like heavy stamens, draw the beating ghosts
that yearn now to be balked,
only then bodied, only then living again.

10   *The Bridge Again*

There is a tweed coat swirling waterlogged,
and there a spar with a clinging rubber glove,
and small darknesses like opening mouths.
These are the satin waters that undress
softly and so many, spendthrift waters.

As to be blinded in the darkness of a stairwell,
or surprise in your reflection one you loved,
or lose in the day the day's unlikeliness,
here the all-foreseen runs swiftly never-done,
yet holds so firmly the image of the moon.

POISON

The tulip indolently cool
left tilted in a glass just to say *This
is the thought I had of you,*

through no one's fault that I can tell,
unpetals, opening
one red door, then two

on Katie, who's knelt at toadstools,
beetles, three leaves glistening
with *Is this poison? Is this poison?*

ever since learning that our fungicide
has the same name, *bluestone,*
as the pebbles whose rich gnashing

means someone coming up the drive.
(Tell: is it the flaw,
desire—or the rule?)

Now in quest of *magic crystals,*
dangerous or true,
whose difference from ordinary gravel

(at least, as far as I can tell)
is in her wanting them, she glances up,
hoping to see no one at all,

because she's wandered almost far enough
to get called.

DEFENSE

And as for my errorless season in center:
from the bat's crack and the angle of reflection
I would gauge the resentment of the hit,
and where it would travel getting over it.

And though I was sprinting flat-out, or laid on the wind
in some bone-breaking dive, it was my study,
for one long moment, always to have been there
(Range subsides to basin; summer, in your moody,

deepening gaze, is Fall; a dream, years long,
happens within the sounding of an alarm.
How kind the night . . .) looking that moon of a ball
with still eyes into the stillness of my hands.

For even the boy who dreams of launching homers
through the outer planets, all contact lost,
saying to the face unmet *I will never need you,*
learns no drive is complete till it is caught.

Till his prayer falls stingless into the mind of god,
and touch, eyes closed, cannot be told from touched,
and in the listening darkness of the glove
it is no more blesséd to give than to receive.

MY YOUNG CARPENTER

"I'm not a man of many words," he says *drack drong*
hammering. Though once, and oftener than once,
"Just married" *thwang* and "Now that I'm married . . ." *throng*.
And when he pauses to breathe, deeply, his hand,
how can my glance up, weeding, fail to comprehend
he is turning his young wife over in his mind:
as many entrances as a half-framed house.
How, in his conjugation, *drenk drank dronk,*
from sheer manyness her beauty is revolving
with duty *drack* and tenderness *tat tat,*
and blind guesses. How sometimes looking down at her:
slowly as darkness climbing to find soft stars,
he enters himself, finally deep, with a sound
like a sanding stroke, or a car's traversing *zwishhhhhh*.

Unlikely his hovering lightness, finishing *det dit*
what he builds for me, deft-jointed, and for himself,
him with no house yet, drawing plans—for a child,
is it? He's not a man of many words: they are
difficult as getting a huge bookcase around
a turn in a narrow hall, and irretrievable.
As for work: there is more time to get it right.
Here a door still doorless, stair still open-mouthed,
the walls so slowly closing out their closing in,
the roof, half weather, on which he is stapling down
tar paper, *pack-it pack-it*. Simple the works of men.

A DISQUISITION UPON THE SOUL

It doesn't register the kid on rollerblades,
or two on the bench that wind sends lightly together,
or the *Times* they leave, or who sleeps under it.
No, those are the heart's. The soul is an old, slow camera
that shows which way the waveless ocean was,
and the day, and darkness, and again the day;
but all things moved or moving, us or ours,
it sees through. Therefore it does not see them.
Is it the restlessness, then, that in the thick of our lives
sends us to windows, wishing for the end
of all that has made us happy? That, sadly,
is also the heart. The soul would not know
which dying friend you thought you could leave for dead,
what shattering love you could leave your daughter for,
or that you stayed, since no one stays long enough;
and, being immortal, hardly knows it was alive
when it is back where it came from after all our years,
as faintly blued as snow is from the height of our skies
and heavier only by the sound of waters.

NINE OAKS

It hadn't seemed so bad from my study—
thronging gutters, struggle of windows, thunder—
but here, nine oaks that were a hall of calm
are hugely uprooted. More than a century,
surely, they had overarched this road
like guarantors of gravity. Now they show
how shallow the roots are that we teeter on,
how much higher, and still higher, the blue
it seems my little car might plummet into.

There are worse catastrophes, Lord knows,
I mutter, half-mad at my tears-on-cue.
Who but blissheads believes in the pain of trees?
(But who believes only what he believes?)
And maybe the rootcloud's helpless paleness
touches, where all losses are the same,
as one glass, rung, sets others thinly singing,
upon the paleness lovers love to find
that shouldn't be out here for every eye
and the damage of light going on and on.

Or maybe these trees, though not our property,
were something I had counted on to stay.
When I was younger, I wanted to hear sages
say everything grows again, to everything its season.
But less of life seems replaceable, now
when the less that's left seems somehow more my own.
Some things I will see again. Things that take time—
great trees, a nation's peace, or a friend's,
or on the white sill just that patient light—
may come back to this life, but not to mine.

MOTHY ODE

One of those pizza-like images of the moons of Jupiter
before computer enhancement is how I look to this moth,
since that's how everything looks (see Monet, etcetera)
before the brain, with help from personal history,
cleans it up. And this moth, the poor trustee
of one small fraction of a thought, has got no room
in its two-byte brain for *This* or *Feed?* or *Breed!*
and *Clean it up* together. And as to history: *Huh?*

So I'm *Bulk, vertical,* joined firmly to the earth,
the same as a bookcase or a tree. This pleases me.
Does a moth see depth? I guess it would have to
to steer boldly among stems to find whatever it finds
(what do moths eat, anyway, nectar? air? ignorance?)

Its life must be a video driving game,
cartoon-like obstacles rising up, its own swerving
difficult to tell from the roads. It can't have room
for the thought *I'm steering* as it steers, giddily,
down the slope of pheromone concentrations
in something that feels like providential falling.
Something thinks *for* it, the moth would think, if it could
               think.

From a moth's angle, I am the sheer heft
of Otherness, in all its inexplicable wonder.
Everything about me is pure instress, startling me-ness,
my gaffes and hesitations wired from birth.
Even the frantic waving of my arms, *Hey Moth!*
seems to declare me a creature of pure nature,
though it looks to me like considerable calculation.

In tragic opposition, some Super-Moth might mourn,
the essence of Mothness is to fixate on high contrast
and, surging again and again (in a kind of software crash)
into romantic candles, or unromantic porchlights,
roast and pulverize. Ah, this is beauty, all the soul can take
of passion's endless loop! Which is not so pleasing.

Whereas a human's amazingly fluid slowness (to a moth)
reveals a being unburdened by desire (like a stone,
I would say, but moths don't notice stones) and wedded,
by a massiveness beyond conception, to the planet,
or, as their apostrophe to us goes,

Anchor,
wind-strayed never,
into no sun falling,
daystander, pure endurer
of the dazzling brilliance of our drives . . .

or something like that, and we who can sit so long,
looking at pages (it seems to them) of darkness,
we with the calm of oceans and things too slow to be visible,
we who are indistinguishable from each other,
how could we suffer reverses? Well may they whirr at my
                    screens

Thou was not born for death, immortal human—
the bulk I see this passing night was seen
by ancient polyphemus, hawkmoth, luna . . .

in ultrasonic worship. Why *shouldn't* I,
since they ask so little, mime, as for my children,
a simplicity that might ease their faith?
The god-part comes so naturally: *O little ones!*
hear my thunderous speech, each word long as a moth-life.
The flame I look upon unmoved. Also the porchlight.

All that your flitteriness leaves ungrasped,
I hold up, practically an Assistant Planet.

I am the blindness with which the Universe
beholds itself and knows itself divine.
I am the huge unmoving root
of that body of which you, O jittery ones,
are the tips of the fingertips, and when I ponder
I grow perfect as darkness, disappearing. There.

FOR THE BIRDS

Where are the songs of Spring? Aye, where are they?
—Keats

The one that says *soothe soothe* to the roofs,
the one that says *3-D 3-D,*
the one that says
(Thoreau says) *drop it drop it,*
the one that makes me look up
thinking it's the brakes of the mail truck.

*

Like a word I've given over
trying to remember, *Spring.*
To say *too soon* too late
or *too late* too soon.

*

One that leers, one that disparages,
the owl we have never seen,
the *skrawk* of drawer.

Is it the redwinged blackbird,
that vocal interbred with metals?

Somebody somebody
owes me a letter.

*

I forked up in half-frozen garden
body or fibrous tuber,

136

beak or seedhusk, was it?
Was it foot or root?
And smoothed it back as hopelessly
(quartz eye or eye?) as when I dreamed
my teeth came out in my hands
like words I could not take back,
or in the silver mirror, slivering,
my wan face fell in petals.

*

whose is the dawn song whose is the dawn
never remembered until heard
whose is the dawn

*

Why should it be important, this smattering of spokes
and snatch of song she passes me with
that, with huge earphones, she can't hear she's singing,
head back, *wah-Wah* and *Wah wah Wah?*
Haven't I known forever: interior is aria,
toes to the stage edge, darkened audience?—
song is not to be heard, song singing
No one is moved as I am by this song.
Why, if I've known forever, *Wah wah Wah*
wah Wah wah is my heart so BRO-o-OO- ken?

*

The quickening ping-pong ball
of *dit* and *dit*
and *dit dit dididit*

a bug? a bird   a bird? a bug (a bird)

*

A pot that has begun to stick,
lump in the throat,
last chink of night,
last rag of snow,
the blot where the printer jammed,
all letters at once—
O little dead thing
that patience will untie,

one thread of CO_2, a rope of sands,
cord of its song,
and miles-long strings of light and water.

*

Whip poor Will
wee-eep wee-eep
chuck Will's widow
why me? why me?

Thus folk imagination
hears narrative or lyric
(do or be done-to)
in anything *re-peated* and *re-peated.*

*

Another head wrapped in an unheard song,
nodding *one,* nodding *one*
like someone waiting for the bus to empty
to get on.

*

Children too elfin to stand still for love,
punctuation without words
(veer of intonation as the sentence ends?)

each an enormous
photon, the flock
only the quantum uncertainty
of one,

how we look to each other,
how I look to myself forgiven,

not saying *you you you*
to anything you come upon.

*

Its wings-flat glide, or better,
its funny little flick,
nearing a branch, to land tight:

grace, I mean, its Indo-European root
of the same tender wood
as *gravity,* as *grief,* as *gratitude.*

*

the one that climbs from peek to pique to peak
the argument: *same same free free*

*

three on a sing
three on a sing
singsong
(sang the singers,

quick stars blown dark
before they burnt God's fingers)

*

(As for the secret english on my English:
inaudible, I've learned, to anyone else:
let it go? What no one else can tell me
how can I stop whispering to myself?)

*

somewhere in the tuliptree
has been will be   has been will be

*

Is this the end the end
one says
        one says
No this is this is

THROUGH AUTUMN

1

On a wooded hillside, staring into woods,
our house is built on a punched-down bulge of fill.
If my eyes could bore through the trees and one more hill
I would see New Jersey's sandy and paler green
flat-out thirty-mile run to the sea—
though for kids like me, who grew up on plains
where the streets are loomed with wires, and the sky is a stare,
not to is the point of buying here.

2

A tortoise and wild turkeys (six),
a luna moth, a great horned owl,
two half-imaginary foxes
we save like passes to the next world.

3

Storms stumble on us, hurrying from the West,
as if there were one more step than they expected,
and in their thrashing fall take down century oaks
and the tops of soft-wooded tulip trees.

In an hour all the rain in town is here
via the doubled and redoubled tumbling stream,
or the conduit we hear licking under the drive,
or the sourceless outburst at the foot of the hill.

Our little glade, technically wetlands, softens,
and the sun pushes out, hammering the damp

into midges finer than any screen
we swab like ash from beneath a left-on lamp.

4

All night, the strange busyness of night,
something desperate wailing *Paul Paul,*
too monotone, we decide, to be a woman.
Mockernuts and acorns swishing down.
Morning, no change, nor any sign
of the paint can or corrugated tin
that one in ten, plummeting, rang like a gong.

5

The expectant trimness of the houses, a reserve
more revealing than confession:
like the perfumed mirror, the straightened dresser
of the room you blunder into, hoping
for your stashed coat when the party's over.

6

I could write a field guide, *Faint Hums of the World,*
distinguishing the subliminal calls
of thermostat and fritzed transformer
from Black Cable Box and Greater Electric Clock
for the benefit of panicky new homeowners
whose bodies are houses, now, whose hearing is larger.
I need to know, lights out, on my loud pillow,
whether it's choral digestion of the gypsy moths
or the cosmic background radiation I hear seething,

or the sound of my own, or of someone else's, listening.
(I pad downstairs to be sure it's nothing).

7

Too many starlings, too many deer
and squirrels. Our little stream
unslurred by algae, disturbingly clear,
supports nothing but waterstriders.
Hardly a toad or warbler, overplus
of honeysuckle, bluejays, lawn:
ecologically shallow, you might say,
the way the soul gets when too busy,
or insisting to itself *I'm happy, I'm happy.*

8

The *clock* of plate on plate,
aspirin's rattle,
the radio's intermittent
nerves of static,

button ticking
and ticking in the dryer,
unballing paper's
crackle, timid fire,

and the click bug—how
it got in, I don't know—
like someone's typing out,
unbearably slow,

of a list. But what is it a list of?

9

In the kitchen, somewhere, but we can't root out
the *inner cricket,* as we call him,
huge-sounding, probably speck-like,
precision almost electronic
in his timing of the year's pure running down.

10

You can hear them in the eaves
like a radio faintly receiving,
or a drink fizzing flatter,
the carpenter bees,
chewing their bullet-round holes:
blunt, black
and stingless, though their lumbering
can unsteady you on a ladder.

11

Blast from the quarry, groundwave first,
shockwave arriving out of step.
Between them all the disasters
I have to remind myself it isn't.

Not a siren: my wind-leaky car's
whistle, like a teapot starting.
Not the door, but a flicker
knocking at a maple gone soft-hearted.

Not the unburied Titans
fumbling in their pockets for loose change,
just the recycling truck, its pouring clash
of metal on metal, glass on glass.

Time after time, Nine Tones,
the gods' names in this age,
are arranged and rearranged.
In their true succession,

(trashcan rattling down the drive,
flicker knocking at the eaves)
something in the day will fling open,
our bodies blow off like leaves.

12

Or how about the carrion beetles,
black and yellow, and so like the panels
of the roadkill turtle they were feasting on,
that for a long minute, while I tasked and tasked
my eyes to stop seeing what they saw, I was sure
the parts were walking away from the whole's disaster?

13

The power bucks, then goes out.
We go by wide-eyed instinct through the house.
Here turn, step, duck, here turn again.
Roughness of wallpaper, dead switch,
the height of a riser, count before the landing,
everything invisible but memory,
firm under our feet, taking our hands.

14

Floor of the study, patch of warm?
Ceiling light on in the room downstairs.

Kitchen floor's wet chill?
Ice chip, melted. Or another of the dead
has walked out of the Great Water.

15

Turn in the stair: the smell
of dinner lingers, bubblegum,
mildew that in some breezeless corner
has resumed doubling.

Since that may be gas,
skip the matches, pass
the mirror darkly,
fearing the flick of a switch
for its tiny blue spark,

or the tiny yellow one
where the key slides into the cylinder,
or your knuckle cracks, or one thought
sets off another.

16

Even the phone ringing
like the long release of rain
when a tree's blown, long after rain,

even the VCR, its bright addition
of 12 and 12 and 12,
even the spreading blue

the pen I fell asleep on shot me with,
even the tick of a downspout, like a heart
forgetting to ask why it keeps count.

Even the sea, in this hour trending
upward the unmeasurable increment
that will have it lapping at our steps
on a November evening, A.D. Twenty Million.

17

Andromeda and fern along the front,
sage and daisies in the backyard's sun.
In the cockeyed, brimming gutter,
salamanders and a seedling tree.
Microclimates: things dig in
exactly where they're supposed to be.

In the brightest window, in the muntin's
sixteenth-inch of shadow, mildew darkens.
Within the shadowy body: deeper shadows,
and shadows within them, favorable enough
that a cell-size shadow repeats and repeats itself.

18

Sparrows raucous in the gutters,
all the contusions of the wind,
sublimation of roof shingles in the moon
will wear a house down.

And nothing destroys a house like confidence.
Understood.
But my anxiety's perfect, I say,
knock-knocking on wood.

19

The raccoon whose custom was to muscle our cans,
was too careless, or too careful, crossing the street,
and lay for a long time upside down,
while whatever was thinking him through slowly concluded
he was reducible to a tooth-white spine.
Like a little drawing of a bridge, I might have added,
and perfectly uncrossed, but whether now
simpler or more difficult I don't know.

20

Bacteria don't know which way is down.
A gnat forgets. Mice fall
unharmed from airliners.
Memo: be small.

21

My daymare is, crossing suspension bridges,
that I'm ordered to build one in the Middle Ages.
I wrack my brains for info about ores,
derive from scratch techniques for smelting,
and analyze the stresses of the catenary.
I have to invent precision tools, but first, precision.
I have to explain, my God, why this is necessary!

22

Someone I can't make out behind the tint
honk-honks. I wave because she thinks I should,
hoping to find out later what I meant.

23

I keep finding in the fur of little tasks
littler tasks,

and in needs, more needs.

How quickly an intuition
becomes a duty,

the faint deer paths
that dirt bikes codify.

24

Antennas waving, button-ended,
where daisies had risen through the slatted seats
of our lawn chairs, a committee in recess,
that I left so carefully in place all summer
as a monument to carelessness.

25

Who frisks me for the hours
I've stolen millions of?
My red alarm says 80:01
or 10:08 (it's upside-down).

26

Disorder chains, but cataclysm frees.
Sighing, I bend for some litter,
but the leaves in crisis, hemispheres of snow
are beyond one man to undo.

27

(Though someone proves that in a dimension n
there's a single point
from which these random-seeming, cross-blown leaves
stream out, rays of a sun . . .)

28

Someone is having trouble with the picture,
pixels at the red end wobbling down.
There is shrilling under the dialogue: crickets.
Someone is having trouble with the sound.

From the rained woods, odor of cigar box.
Someone walks through an ember the size of a city.
He suffers uncued tears, the sky's too *sky*.
We apologize for our technical difficulties.

Someone feels like he's walking on a bed
high pillowy and underwater steps,
someone's a wind, he says, with nothing to blow.
Baffling, this glitch in proprioception.

Someone is having trouble with his sequence,
flashback, ellipsis, work-around,
who muffs his big line, *Spare me O death,*
ad-libbing *Come down, whatever, O come down!*

29

In the woods, the soft fall
of the year on the year before.

Deer of evening, browsing, growing bluer.
Who is that at your shoulder but the sun
or someone offering you a mild, gold drink?

30

This midge is a geometer,
driven or deft,
who squares off, eye-level,
turning left and left and left.

Sphere of cabbage whites? Electrons.
Sparrow on glass? A blurted explanation.
The threshing of the deer in leaves
is a child's unwrapping of a package—

and all this accidental happiness,
so simple
that it looks like fate? A sentence
I began at twenty-one with "For example. . . . "

31

And, after all, the guy who admonished us
Don't buy a stick of furniture, or paint
until you have watched four seasons in a house
must have thought all the art in living
was not to live, but to make a place forever.
Perfection's to sell. Happiness, let go:
let the window be a wall, the wall a window.

32

A poor man's cow dies, a rich man's child:
so the archaic proverb goes, unkind
unless the poor man, dreaming that being known
for what he is will bring him all he deserves,
and the rich one, dreading he will be found
to have, already, more than he deserves
are the same man, rich with loss,
the transparent house within my house,
the empty road that shrills within my roads,
that I cannot live with, cannot live without.

33

Squirrels can circle what we call our lot
at roof-height without ever touching down,
since the trees reach one into another,
shaped deeply by their standing together.

In sharp distinction, solitary trees
approximate their field guide forms,
and poplar is purely poplar or elm elm,
which makes for a half-truth in our human realm:

the soul that blurs in a morning on the phone
grows mirror-clear when I am an hour alone,
sure—but what day, what field's so spacious
that I could unimagine imagination,
and walk out to the middle and be only myself,
not forming your words in my head, not hearing you listen?

34

This evening blue knows everything:
one house and disappearing trees.
It would let me stand for everyone,
but I am tired of its tired anonymous tenderness,
its meaning silence, its universal condescension.

Someone is burning road-chunks against the cold.
Someone's pillow is stuffed with maple leaves.
No one can turn his life into another's.
No one can take his riches with him, or his burdens.
Neither rich nor poor shall pass through the eye of the needle.

35

High squirrel against the sun, all haze and blaze,
and loud,
a creature interrupted in its metamorphosis
from tree to cloud.

36

I have seen foot-long fish sailing in the trees
where Millstone rose and left them to blister.

I have seen that the grass is a herd,
slowly turning as the wind turns,

and how dry it is under the roads
and heavy for what lives there.

I have felt in the body fronts and swarms,
now, in autumn, on the move,

and deep in the pool of night the milky blur
of the galaxy's swung arm.

37

Under the sky so huge and restless,
what can we do
but, like the astonished trees,
look up, let go,

all of us tourists at the duty-free,
dropping our last words in the language,
last of our currency.

Now the ripe incapable squirrels
squandered under our tires,
and the slick of leaves,

we drive with swift indifference over the desires
that drove us yesterday,
somehow garish and irrelevant already
as if we were puzzling over them ten years later.

38

Too many years to figure by trial and error
whether it's orange juice or exercise,
the succor of a jay or dumb luck
that saves you, which is the prime hour of the day
for wit or prayer, speed or desire,
or which of your dreams of love go all the way.
No experiment can prove you right or wrong:
too many variables, controls insufficient.
After a time, there's no time for experience.

39

Each instrument of our kitchen,
each handle in my garage
is part of a god who broke up, as gods do,
into aspects—the screwer, the smoother,
the divider into equal streams—
in the storm of prayer reduced to his uses.

Our stories ran out, yes. The story: goes on.
Isn't it art
to find the second use of ourselves, compulsion gone?

40

Now it's just crickets: little
files, drills, hammers.
Nothing sadder, lovelier
than their *bleak* and *bleak*
thinning the fields
the sad heart must have wanted thinner.

41

These are the skies, the waters, kindly metals.
These are the mums, like cliff fires in the mist,
August-fired, jagged happenings
that hardiness has made indelicate.

Now the milkweed rattles and the burdock
harboring the last crickets, counting down,
everywhere late oxides of a beauty
hardly less beautiful as it browns.

The squirrel panics to the curb, the cyclist
hunches, sneaking between the winds,
I drive home wronged, no, wrong—blue twilight
a premature hypothesis.

Day I worked for, just now looking up?
No one mentioned it had come and gone.
Not leaves: it's vision that lets go and blows.
O gravity, divinely video!

And will the mind, mid-winter,
be small as I remember:
noon, the breadth of a windshield;
midnight, lit circle on a letter?

These are the geese, bad oboists,
that one bright gene, vestigial,
remembers how to translate: *all regret*.

Ah Life! But we can live without it.

VECTORS:
Aphorisms & Ten-Second Essays (2001)

1. The road reaches every place, the shortcut only one.

2. Those who demand consideration for their sacrifices were making investments, not sacrifices.

3. What you give to a thief is stolen.

4. Despair says *I cannot lift that weight.* Happiness says, *I do not have to.*

5. You've never said anything as stupid as what people thought you said.

6. Our avocations bring us the purest joys. Praise my salads or my softball, and I am deified for a day. But tell me I am a great teacher or a great writer and you force me to tell myself the truth.

7. Ah, what can fill the heart? But then, what *can't?*

8. Shadows are harshest when there is only one lamp.

9. Desire's most seductive promise is not pleasure but change, not that you might possess your object but that you might become the one who belongs with it.

10. I say nothing works any more, but I get up and it's tomorrow.

11. A beginning ends what an end begins.

12. I walk up the drive for the morning paper and find myself musing, as if the news were fiction, *Marvelous that they think of all this, so deadpan strange.* Nothing is so improbable as the truth. If the day's headlines hadn't already happened, they would not happen.

13. Gravity's reciprocal: the planet rises to the sparrow's landing.

14. When a jet flies low overhead, every glass in the cupboard sings. Feelings are like that: choral, not single; mixed, never pure. The

sentimentalist may want to deny the sadness or boredom in his happiness, or the freedom that lightens even the worst loss. The moralist will resist his faint complicity. The sophisticate, dreading to be found naive, will exclaim upon the traces of vanity or lust in any motive, as if they were the whole. Each is selling himself simplicity; each is weakened with his fear of weakness.

15.   Road: what the man of two minds travels between them.

16.   The cynic suffers the form of faith without its love. Incredulity is his piety.

17.   Pessimists live in fear of their hope, optimists in fear of their fear.

18.   Writer: how books read each other.

20.   If the couple could see themselves twenty years later, they might not recognize their love, but they would recognize their argument.

21.   Each lock makes two prisons.

22.   Painting high on the house. Yellow jackets swarmed around me. I couldn't convince them I was harmless, so I had to kill them.

23.   All stones are broken stones.

24.   Of all the ways to avoid living, perfect discipline is the most admired.

25.   Why would we write if we'd already heard what we wanted to hear?

26.   It is by now proverbial that every proverb has its opposite. For every *Time is money* there is a *Stop and smell the roses*. When someone says *You never stand in the same river twice* someone else has already replied *There is nothing new under the sun*. In the mind's arithmetic, 1 plus −1 equals 2. Truths are not quantities but scripts: *Become for a moment the mind in which this is true.*

29. Pain is not a democracy.

32. If you're Larkin or Bishop, one book a decade is enough. If you're not? More than enough.

33. No gift is ever exactly right for me. But why do I suppose the gift is for me, or my gratitude for the giver?

34. Where I touch you lightly enough, there I am also touched.

35. It's easy to renounce the world till you see who picks up what you renounced.

37. As much innocence is found as lost.

38. The world is not what anyone wished for, but it's what everyone wished for.

39. The will is weak. Good thing, or we'd succeed in governing our lives with our stupid ideas!

40. Wind cannot blow the wind away, nor water wash away the water.

41. If you do everything for one reason, then all you have done will become meaningless when the reason does.

43. Do we return again and again to our losses to get back what we had or lose what remains?

45. I have to start over and over on the loves and books that most possess me, so fine the difference is between knowing and not knowing them.

46. We invent a great Loss to convince ourselves we have a beginning. But loss is a current: the coolness of one side of a wet finger held up, the faint hiss in your ears at midnight, water sliding over the dam at the back of your mind, memory unremembering itself.

47. Looking back: youth, innocence, energy, desire. But none of it's as amazing as all we were sure we *had to do*.

49. No matter who you love, you make love to a woman and a man.

50. Not beauty, not even need. We fall in love because we are unused —the less used, the more foolishly we fall.

51. Of all our self-delusions, none is more exhausting or transparent than that of our indispensability. But it keeps telling us we are generous to remain deceived.

52. Value yourself according to the burdens you carry, and you will find everything a burden.

54. Patience is not very different from courage. It just takes longer.

56. In clearing out files, ideas, hopes, throw away a little too much. Pruning only dead wood will not encourage growth.

57. It's not that reason kills faith; reason is the lesser faith that steers us when we have already lost a greater one.

60. The saints and the sinners say the same thing about life: *Only for a moment.*

62. Of course we're enraged when Authority bores us: that right we give only to our intimates.

63. I have to deserve my joys. So do my enemies. For those I love, my standards are more sensible.

64. God help my neighbors if I loved them as I love myself.

68. The poem in the quarterly is sure to fail within two lines: flaccid, rhythmless, hopelessly dutiful. But I read poets from strange languages

with freedom and pleasure because I can believe in all that has been lost in translation. Though all works, all acts, all languages are already translation.

69. The tyrant has first imagined he is a victim.

71. We do not love money. But once we have it, it is not *money*. It is *ours*.

72. Millions of perfect crimes are committed every day, by no one.

74. You can't pretend you're just watching the actors. Someone a little further away will see you acting the part of a watcher.

75. On what is valuable thieves and the law agree.

77. The tyrant puts down his own rebellion, everywhere.

79. Desire, make me poor again.

80. Success repeats itself until it is failure.

82. If it can be used again, it is not wisdom but theory.

84. In the long run, the single sin is less of a problem than the good reasons for it.

89. For each thing we do to change, we do a million to remain the same.

93. Wind, ocean, fire: the things we like to liken our passions to don't break, can't stop.

94. My weaknesses are less remarkable than all the things I have at one time or another imagined were my strengths.

95. You do not have to be a fire to keep one burning.

97.   *But for this rock,* its shadow says, *I could get at the sun.*

99.   We wouldn't take so many chances if we really believed in chance.

106.   The wound hurts less than your desire to wound me.

107.   Those who are too slow to be intelligent deserve our patience, those who are too quick, our pity.

108.   Think of all the smart people made stupid by flaws of character. The finest watch isn't fine long when used as a hammer.

112.   The first abuse of power is not realizing that you have it.

113.   Education is so slow, disorganized, accidental that sometimes it seems I could have relaxed for forty years and then learned everything I know in a few months of really efficient study. Then again, I'm not sure what I know.

114.   Greater than the temptations of beauty are those of method.

116.   If I didn't spend so much time writing, I'd know a lot more. But I wouldn't know anything.

118.   Everyone has the same secrets. That is the secret we keep best.

119.   You will know the real god by your fear of loving it.

120.   Only the dead have discovered what they cannot live without.

122.   To think yourself incapable of crime is one failure of imagination. To think yourself capable of all crimes is another.

123.   Theories of happiness are somehow less troubled by the misfortunes of the deserving than by all those people who are happy and couldn't possibly be.

128. Intimates: the ones it's hardest to tell everything you're thinking.

130. Actions speak louder than words. But how I say is what I do.

131. Harder to laugh at the comedy if it's about you, harder to cry at the tragedy if it isn't.

133. Even at the movies, we laugh together, we weep alone.

136. Loving your enemies takes away their right to hate you. Kinder to endure being the enemy they need.

137. Tragic hero, madman, addict, fatal lover. We exalt those who cannot escape their fates because we cannot stay inside our own.

138. No one desired is unchanged: the god of many cannot remain the true god.

141. There might have been a god before Creation, but by now he must be bewildered in all our suffering and fantasy, like a man in a dream he cannot remember to wake up from.

142. Growth is barely controlled damage.

144. Why would they need Realism if they were sure they were real?

150. They say productivity is the key to confidence, and confidence. . . to productivity. And they're happy walking back and forth between these two rooms, each the excuse for the other.

151. I sell my time to get enough money to buy it back.

152. Addiction, profession, virtue. Anything is a game if its rules are simpler than time's.

154. Only eternity needs eternity. But without the year, no growth; without the hour, no love; without the second, no grace, no thought.

157. *I'll buy that* means also *I believe it.* Your choices: spend, and believe in things; save, and believe in money.

160. When I want to change myself, I invent a new rule, like a revolutionist who has discovered he believes neither in freedom nor in those he intended to free.

162. Everyone loves the Revolution. We only disagree on whether it has occurred.

163. A day is only a day. But a life is only a life.

164. The hard of hearing cannot tell their voices are loud.

168. No price fluctuates so wildly as that of time.

170. To be sincere is one thing. To practice Sincerity is to burden everyone else with believing you.

171. To know, you just have to know. To believe, you have to make others believe.

174. Debts of a certain immensity demand betrayal.

175. Do not blame the fire for knowing one thing.

176. When it rains you discover which things you did not want out in the rain.

179. Every life is allocated one hundred seconds of true genius. They might be enough. If we could just be sure which ones they were.

183. I know which disasters could be mine by how dangerous pity is.

186. Absence makes the heart grow fonder: then it is only distance that separates us.

187. If you want to know how they could forget you, wait till you forget them.

191. *Throw it away.* But there is no *away.*

194. No matter how fast you travel, life walks.

195. The best way to know your faults is to notice which ones you accuse others of.

196. To condemn your sin in another is hypocrisy. Not to condemn is to reserve your right to sin.

197. Let me have my dreams but not what I dream of.

204. By looking for the origins of things we deceive ourselves about their inevitability. Things that did not happen also have origins.

205. Who would be slave to his passions if they did not also feel like freedom?

206. What we talked ourselves out of was a whim. What we did *anyway* was a passion. So it seems now. But later, how confusing the difference between passion and predictability. And the thing we felt free to dismiss comes to seem our freedom.

207. Sometimes I hate beauty because I don't have any choice about loving it. I must be wrong in this, but whether because I take freedom too seriously, or love, I cannot tell.

208. If you change your mind, you are free. Or you were.

212. Happiness is not the only happiness.

216. The mistakes I made from weakness embarrass me far less than those I made insisting on my strength.

219.   It takes more than one life to be sure what's killing you.

221.   More than you remember stays green all winter.

222.   Worry wishes life were over.

224.   Water deepens where it has to wait.

225.   Minds go from intuition to articulation to self-defense, which is what they die of.

227.   I am saving good deeds to buy a great sin.

230.   Some things, like faith, cheer, courage, you can give when you do not have them.

233.   If I belch at the table I am embarrassed. But not so much if no one hears. Or if you pretend not to have heard. Or I pretend I do not know you heard. Or you pretend you do not know I know.

234.   Why should the whole lake have the same name?

237.   How much less difficult life is when you do not want anything from people. And yet you owe it to them to want something.

241.   Self-love, strange name. Since it feels neither like loving some-one, nor like being loved.

242.   If I can keep giving you what you want, I may not have to love you.

245.   Who gives his heart away too easily must have a heart under his heart.

247.   It's amazing that I sit at my job all day and no one sees me clearly enough to say *What is that boy doing behind a desk?*

248. Who breaks the thread, the one who pulls, the one who holds on?

254. Idolaters of the great need to believe that what they love cannot fail them, adorers of camp, kitsch, trash that they cannot fail what they love.

255. No criticism so sharp as seeing they think you need to be flattered.

256. Time heals. By taking even more.

261. Turn on the light and you will see, but it will not be darkness that you see.

262. Competition and sympathy are joined at the root, as may be seen in the game *My grief is greater than yours,* which no one can keep himself from playing.

263. How fix the unhappy couple, when it was happiness they loved in each other?

264. After a while of losing you, I become the one who has lost you. Did the pain change me, or did I change to lessen the pain?

265. Experience tends to immunize against experience, which is why the most experienced are not the wisest.

266. The mind that's too sensitive feels mostly itself. A little hardness makes us softer for others.

273. You who have proved how much like me you are: how could I trust you?

276. No garden without weeds? No weeds without gardens.

277. Memory's not infinite. If I looked at this pitted and pocked wall microscopically enough the visual data would fill my brain entirely.

Against this, boredom and reflex generalization protect me. If I call up the wall in memory, some generic version will be made up—I never see *nothing,* I never see gaps or error messages where I have forgotten or mistaken. Same even with those cherished early memories: we call up a sketch, fill in the blanks, and store it again, changed. There is no virgin past. The mind is like one of those floating islands of vegetation whose roots grasp not the earth but each other.

284.   Believe stupid praise, deserve stupid criticism.

285.   I need a much larger vocabulary to talk to you than to talk to myself.

288.   Determinism. How romantic to think the mind a machine reliable enough to transform the same causes over and over again into the same effects. When even toasters fail!

289.   No use placing mystical trust in the body. It is perfectly adapted to life a million years ago *Eat while you can, flee, strike.* But what does it know about cities, love, speculation? Nor will evolution change it, since failure now leads not to death and subtraction from the gene pool but merely to misery.

291.   If I didn't have so much work to keep me from it, how would I know what I wanted to do?

292.   It gets harder and harder to be free. Every time I need a larger labor to be at the end of.

297.   While everyone clamored at the god, I kept aloof, scorning their selfishness. Now that he has ascended, I hate him because he does not guess what I want.

306.   When you laughed at me, I could have been free, but instead of laughing with you, I clung to my imprisonment.

307.   Do not ask the roads whether it is good to travel.

312. I could explain, but then you would understand my explanation, not what I said.

316. The road forgets what's underneath the road.

318. The obvious was not necessarily obvious before you heard it.

322. How strong my weakness is!

323. I keep glimpsing the loneliness I want, my thoughts without me.

325. The best disguise is the one everyone else is wearing.

327. Believe everything a little. The credulous know things the skeptical do not.

335. No matter how much time I save, I have only now.

336. Pleasure is for you. Joy is for itself.

337. The dead are still writing. Every morning, somewhere, is a line, a passage, a whole book you are sure wasn't there yesterday.

338. The happy and the suffering probably understand life equally well, but the sufferers may see a little more clearly how little it is that they understand.

339. Everywhere he looked Nerval saw a black spot. That one's easy, but where the optic nerve enters the retina there is another one, quite literally a blind spot. We never notice: the brain, like a mother softening the bad news, continually fills it in, never letting us know there is nothing there. O, spot I never see, from you I learn my landscapes are movies, my words a greeting card, my memories an official explanation!

341. There are silences harder to take back than words.

344.   To paranoids and the Elect everything makes sense.

349.   The man who sticks to his plan will become what he used to want to be.

350.   No debt burdens like the fear of debt.

351.   Those who pride themselves on always telling the truth generally concentrate on truths more painful to others than to themselves.

352.   Laziness is the sin most willingly confessed to, since it implies talents greater than have yet appeared.

353.   If we were really sure we were one of a kind, there would be no envy. My envy demeans both of us—no wonder it is the hardest sin to confess. It says I am not who I think I am unless I have what you have. It says that you are what you have, and I could have it.

355.   Envy is ashamed of itself. If it weren't hanging back, it would go all the way to emulation and love.

356.   You would think we would envy only what we love, for being loveable. But no, we envy those the world loves, because we care less for being worthy of love than being loved.

358.   I have so much trouble choosing that I wish restaurants would ask me for a list of things I absolutely will not eat, and then select a dish at random from the rest. In that case, I would only have to figure out how it was good in itself, and not why I again failed to know what would make me happiest.

360.   When my friend does something stupid, he is just my friend doing something stupid. When I do something stupid, I have deeply betrayed myself.

365.   Your hatred is a night bombardment, lighting places of myself I never see. But even in the pain of admitting my selfishness there is

curiosity and relief. To be a character, at last, and a rather ordinary one, from whom I realistically needn't expect too much!

369. Why shouldn't you read this the way I wrote it, with days between the lines?

373. Embarrassment is the greatest teacher, but since its lessons are exactly those we have tried hardest to conceal from ourselves, it may teach us, also, to perfect our self-deception.

376. You keep track of your worth on some wildly cyclic stock market that will soar in fantasy, crash at a cold glance. Other people think you never change.

377. If only we were satisfied to have others think of us what we think of them.

378. I never go to the mirror unless there's something I am hoping not to see.

381. What exhausts imagination is fear of exhausting it. The gods detest hoarders, giving nothing to those who do not trust them to give.

390. The best time is stolen time.

387. Why would we worry what others think of us if their opinions did not change us.

391. What we usually call laziness is undeclared anxiety. Real laziness comes from the angels.

393. Get fat and you will call hunger one of the virtues.

394. As hard as other people are to talk to, I'm glad I don't have to sit next to myself.

395.   Disillusionment is also an illusion.

396.   That I have thought all the evil thoughts does not mean they are mine.

399.   Say nothing as if it were news.
404.   I lust for more strangeness because I have turned everything too easily into myself.

405.   Say too soon what you think and you will say what everyone else thinks.

409.   I am hugely overpaid. Except compared to the people I work with.

413.   Sexiness dates. Beauty, on the other hand, does well with a touch of the archaic: it does not need us.

414.   Disease is whatever tries to turn us into itself.

417.   What were you like back then? Better to look at the young than trust your memory.

419.   I need to blame pain. If you did nothing to deserve it, there is no way I can avoid it. And if I'm the one in pain, better to blame myself than doubt I can escape by doing something right.

424.   The hawkers of self-help tell you to simplify yourself to confidence, optimism, positive feeling. Every time you hear a knock it will be you, selling yourself to yourself.

426.   If they say *It's unique* they want you to buy. If you think *I'm unique* you're trying to sell.

435.   Truth is like the flu. I fight it off, but it changes in other bodies and returns in a form to which I am not immune.

436.   You can't smell what the guests smell.

440.   Bitterness is a greater failure than failure.

449.   Hasn't there, once or twice, been a little too much zeal in our reproof of children and friends for yielding to the temptations we ourselves find it most difficult to resist? We punish where we can least afford to sympathize. Of all the horrors of the daily news, it seems hardest to imagine the kind of cruelty that is intensified by the pain of its victims, but whenever we feel sympathy would weaken us, we are a little closer to the torturer.

458.   Is it an answer, the Silence, or a question?

460.   Opacity gives way. Transparency is the mystery.

465.   Only half of writing is saying what you mean. The other half is preventing people from reading what they expected you to mean.

466.   Easy to criticize yourself, harder to agree with the criticism.

467.   What happens, it is asked, to all the promising young? They promise what *we* wanted; they become what *they* wanted.

469.   All work is the avoidance of harder work.

475.   We have secrets from others. But our secrets have secrets from us.

480.   The lessons of one decade become the innocence of the next.

481.   Our lives get complicated because complexity is so much simpler than simplicity.

490.   Birds are amazing, newspapers, stoves, friends. All that happens is amazing, if you think about it. All that doesn't happen is even more amazing, because there's so much more of it. Only habit keeps us from seeing all this. Habit is really amazing.

493.   The future would be easier to wait for if we could be sure it wasn't already happening.

495.   What happened to the years? How did I get this way? By being this way.

496.   Who, after all, can say *The life I lived was not my life?*

498.   What I hope for is more hope.

499.   To feel an end is to discover that there had been a beginning. A parenthesis closes that we hadn't realized was open).

500.   *All things in moderation,* wisdom says. And says last *Do not be too wise.*

INTERGLACIAL:

New Poems and Aphorisms (2004)

I.

MONSTER MOVIES

SPELLBOUND

And what of the child Bad Magic
clanged shut in a bluebird,
who sat half-lit in the re-leafing arbor,
listening for his old name in the family hubbub,
who meant to cry out . . . but seedflash, hammer of wings . . .
couldn't hold to his dream,
small and quick as a spark, of having been
a child once? Who couldn't see into those windows,
quick as sparks, where slowly they still played,
who meant . . . but shrill, but two flights twined
outflinging. . . . And sometimes in the clatter
of coffee on the lawn, their voices lowering
and slowed (that he could not tell
from landslide, from preliminary thunder),
they would seem to speak of him
something . . . but it was years
and he meant . . . but too-swift heart,
flit like forget and South like a soft downstairs,
and something sang him something flew him away. . . .

MY GODZILLA

Much of the monster movie was (bah DUMMM)
suspense. The coastal fog, the lo-rez video.
You couldn't see him, he was going to be worse than anything,
worse than your worst fears, namely . . .
how could they be your worst if you could know?
Forty years on: you're pretty sure what's coming.
He pokes from the distressingly fragile harbor,
black-tiled, sky-scraping penis, looking a little worse,
for having been nuked and long under water,
but not bad for a penis. *Who's going to clean it up?*
you think, that mess he's making. Also,
that it's fine, his stomping through the gridlock
with a distinctly rubbery wobble,
swatting the haze of planes, drop-kicking taxis.
So maybe he'll snack on the falsetto lovers?
The script, alas, is not what time re-writes.
He's how you look in your bathrobe in the morning,
how you keep smashing through the day,
fired at, invisibly hurt, intent,
litter of ages swirling around your ankles,
the *grit grit grit* of your soles, those tiny, unheard cries.

COLLATERAL DAMAGE

Always they have tumbled from a great height
into the rubble, akimbo, agape.
If they were awake, they'd be kidding;
if dreaming, you'd be embarrassed
at what they've exposed.
How can we forgive them, these wronged ones,
for saying our world is unjust, and dragging
limp children into it, and wailing relatives,
and the hysterical News? They who died
of listening so credulously to the explosion
with the livid ear of their bodies:
Ah, maybe if they'd learned how to behave,
what to brush off, how to keep to themselves
those lilies of their interiors,
color of turnpike sunsets, towels,
garish desire. How demanding they are,
these dead, how impossible
to douse, their loud, loud scarlets,
impossible to keep lit.

THE POOR

Once, as Inuit legend has it,
people became animals, animals people
just by wishing. What a world it was:
lightning of strangeness, luxury of motion!
How in that fishflash
falconfall and silken ottering
of flesh refractable as sunlight
instants of despair persisted
is hard to imagine, yet they must have,
since, as the story continues, one by one
souls wished to be stones, gold, driftwood,
wishless things they could not wish back from,
and this part must be true, since,
look: trillions of them!

As for the few of us
remaining, maybe our souls,
like maps repeatedly refolded,
have gone limp and lost their gift.
Or maybe, and this would be sadder,
we're busy, so deafened with our riches
it all seems poverty and silence
we're scuffing through: desert cities,
pigeons, ratty herds, and (there
but for the grace of God) those stones.
Whose cries and prayers, wintry
or cracked or childlike, we won't hear,
wishing, not even hearing that we wish,
to stay this one sad thing we're sure we are.

MONSTER MOVIES

Martians, Green Knight, serpent that rings the planet,
the gods themselves: in Chapter One,
the enemy's unstoppable, whether his taste
is interspecies sex and shorefront real estate
or vaporizing billions in their pj's.

It's over, wails the populace, but we know better.
The runtime's three-plus hours. There must be something—
rhinovirus, Kryptonite, a magic noodle,
dark secrets that were somehow overlooked.
And this is a Story: someone will be talking.

Take, for example, *Independence Day.*
Spunky earthlings, hacking the dead-black saucer
of the unutterably cruel and powerful invader,
boldly tap out CONNECT on their laptop,
and they're IN. This wouldn't work at the office,

but transgalactic software is so feature-rich,
so powerfully user-friendly, it's defenseless,
wants what you want, and don't know you want,
in love with failure. Which jibes, you'll notice,
with your personal experience of omnipotence:

how it's anxious at heart, unworthy, aw-shucksing,
control-freaking, knocking on wood, already pierced
with the tiny screws of its own screwing up.
There's always an unlocked door that Doom slips through,
a locked door Doom seeps quietly under.

Yes, even the omniscient, telepathic godling
nods, blurring my plot, one channel in trillions,

with his own faint wish to destroy himself.
My noisy ascent of the trellis to his window
with the fated plastic knife between my teeth?—

how can he tell it from his ancient patricide,
a burglar in Santa Barbara, or a holly leaf
scratching a pane next week in Orono?
Poor god, poor me. Our sorriness is equal.
Telepathy, after all, is bidirectional.

Or take Zeus, with his predilection for thunderbolts,
his chronic lust—tuning out for centuries on end
because he had a jealous wife to explain to,
a passel of children quarreling and scheming,
and a planet of complaint singing in his ears.

He wasn't sufficiently focused on omnipotence,
which ideally doesn't limit itself through actions,
so that his myriad powers, inevitably conflicting,
materialized as lesser gods, became weaknesses,
narratives, and (fatally) rumors of Incarnation.

The Story starts, that is, and your strength is strengthless.
Forget slaughtering the babes, or swallowing them,
affecting a heel plate, banishing the princess—
you might as well retire and enjoy the family.
To succeed? Don't ask that oracle in the first place.

Furnish yourself, instead, with an arctic fortress
and a secret identity. Exhibit no powers
beyond those of ordinary mortals. And if you can't will
what's going to happen anyway, at least shut up:
the strong gods are the ones we have never heard of.

END OF THE WORLD

Only for years faint *hush hush* in the walls
and in the off TV
of wings as large as pages,
powder of taupe and umber on glass doors,
then suddenly on the window,
Cecropia—last seen when?—
named for the king who taught burial of the dead.
It's the mask of a god,
his face the size of a cat's,
colorless where the eyes are, or is it
faint silver of the galactic core
feeding on stars?
Hermes, I think, with his decennial message,
patron of liars and speed, but saying
slowly and truly
how strange the gods are, that this
is no mask but his very face,
depthless, unreadable,
more like a hand
clenching on skylines, white powder
streaming from the fist
that does not see what it does.

WORLD NEWS TONIGHT

Now it's evening, blue with the News
we flip on, according to statistics,
to see what's followed us home
from our day of mistakes
like paper cuts, like minutes, tiny but wounding.

That's how they fly, the cruise missiles,
painstakingly, with such care for the detail
of river and double yellow, homing in
on the crossing guard's white glove,
pencil shavings, the letter *r*.

That's not our neighborhood, odds are,
smartly bombed, the bike shop twisted,
not our daughter looking out, wide-eyed
as if she were reading. Why can't she hear us urging
This way, this way . . . we're alive, alive. . . .

IN BLACK AND WHITE

O God, what Lucy's not telling Ricky.
That she's gone down on his clarinetist—
how else get cash?— because she *had* to know
how that tiara and falsies got in his briefcase,
and PI's don't come cheap, and who,
who could just *ask*? And what's gotten in
to Beaver is harder to figure, or My Little Margie.
Yet we stayed in the room with them, cringing,
because they are realer than the News, aren't they,
the things we haven't told each other all these years,
the things I haven't told myself, the plotlessness
that's dumber than their plots. Only the speed was fictional
with which they set up and let fall their schemes
so we could see: they come in the same types we do.
Sage, lover, saint, and fool and fool. But them
we could forgive. How much they made
of the simple hands they were dealt,
their cars all black, their houses white, with what gusto
they clicked at their meals of three fine grays.

STILL LIFE WITH MOVING FIGURE

Was it a *Twilight Zone,* or what,
where time stopped for everyone but him,
and he galloped, dismayed and free,
among the frozen traffic, the on-tiptoe crowds,
manikins they looked like, or photos of themselves?
It was a kid's dream, I knew, even as a kid:
he could have whatever he wanted, the money, the food,
and read with his soft flash all night long,
whatever of their bodies he could learn alone
(but weren't their eyes moving a little?— if they woke up
he better not be anywhere he wasn't supposed to).
Though here's what physics says: if time had really stopped,
those bodies would be less pierceable than stone,
stone hems unlifting in a still wind, also stone,
that would lock him in place like the rest of them.
That's what he's finally getting, wide-eyed,
slowing, when he stares straight out at us,
us three kids, still there after all these years,
motionless in the gray gaze of TV
like stones in a soft strange water,
seeing at last the hard thing he was seeing.

VIRGIN AND SON

January 2000

I passed them in the summer. Now,
glass ceiling shattered, sharp leaves down,
the sky's a millennium higher.
So disproportioned is their sculpting,
or so changed my sense of grace,

that I can't tell:
is it the infant or the crucified god
she cradles, almost slipping from her gaze—
of pity, is it, or adoration?—
so large he is, or so small.

ALL THE GHOSTS

Their dream decelerates the spinning planet
one millimeter-per-second per century,
until, our slowness slowly matching theirs,
they can stride into our lives and live again—

a matter of eons, nothing to them, so patient,
since the massed wish of all the dead
is only the slide of a hem across a floor
or the difference on your face of milder air.

It is their fate, they murmur. It is anyway their way
to shun the theatrical or gothic gesture.
They would not rattle chains if chains could hold them.
It is the wind, so much stronger, that slams doors.

They are heard, if ever, in the dramas of your dreams
where you cannot tell still voices from your own,
intervening, if at all, in the neural substrate,
shunting a lone electron *Maybe* or *Maybe not.*

Theirs are evasive and oblique persuasions,
stone by stream, for example, snows on outer planets,
undetected constants haunting physicists,
eddies where time runs sidelong or remembers.

Their delight is yielding, wind within the wind,
to faint velleities or fainter chances,
for they find among death's consolations, few enough,
the greatest is, to be mistaken for what happens.

When your eyes widen, they are surging to observe
the evening's trend to mauve, and all you have chosen
so slowly you are unaware of choosing.
And you may feel them feel, amused or touched

(history has not been long enough to decide which),
when your blunt patience emulates their own,
when you sense, like them, all fate might well be focused
in the exact glint of a right front hoof uplifted,

when you wait, as they must, for that crisis of precision
when it will make all the difference in the world
whether a particular petal's sideslipping fall
hushes the rim of a glass, or misses.

FRICTIONS

On a slow Tuesday in the distant future
(which in the story was 2004)
they solve at last the mystery of friction.
Nothing would ever grind to a halt, get heated,
no energy would be wasted anywhere.
At last perpetual motion sighed the engineers,
and their sigh sent sagebrush skittering through westerns
and beers tobogganing down endless bars
into the horizon, and a drunk swung wildly,
windmilling on his heel forever
so windily the sigh came round the world
to the engineers, who sighed anew *O saints
of perpetual motion.*
                          A push as light as a wish,
and *whish,* you were on your way forever
since automobiles ran with 100% efficiency
though they blew sideways weightlessly
in the faintest wind, in sighs, like newspapers
or sagebrush, clinging to chainlink fences
or collecting in low spots, churning uselessly
with leaves and tennis balls, with pedestrians,
everything stalled by the slightest incline.

Nothing, if I remember, rested where we put it.
Drawers of their own wills opened, letters.
Hands failed to warm each other. When we sat to talk
our gazes met and slid, if I remember.
Chairs, ballpoints rolled away, and storms rolled in.
Rain would not stick to windows, rise in stems.
My endless notes sublimed in a fine blue mist.

What I remember is sitting tensed and graspless
with the story I never finished, open somewhere,
that could neither endure my touch nor touch me,
waiting, I think it was, to be imagined,
for someone or the wind to turn the page.

SF

The sun is redder in this era, cooler,
noon bronze as sunset was, with early stars.
We're billions of years in the future
so I'm dead, but still reading.

There's not a word of how my last hour went
or which of us died first. As for our children
and our children's children:
I'm beyond all that.

*

It's the heyday of positronic Sentients.
They catch each other's eyes across the vastness
and, lost in broadband gazes of desire,
enact in one delirious zeptosecond
all possible scenarios
with umbrellas and restaurants,
whimsical punchlines, endearing hangups.
and the two of them falling at last and laughing
into fluent digital mixing, ecstatic unity.
In which they forget utterly who they ever were,
or why they wanted, and from which
only one wakes, knowing everything
in a world it has somehow never been in,
and is completely alone.

*

Billions of stories, billions,
too long to listen to, much less to live.

*

The galaxy's been conquered and abandoned.
We've all come home
from weary stars, weary careers
to stay up late in the mild red glow.

What's on is reruns
of those lost, lost years:
hurries and failures.
The usual. But my excuses

are billions of years old,
billions,
and the android waiters
are infinitely bland, and patient.

Say again why it was
you didn't
do what you wanted,
know what you loved?

*

So difficult to tell myself from the future
that I stay up later and later, dead but reading.

GHOST STORY

That flash in the corner of your eye—imaginary?—
that knocking—or was it your heart?—that made you hurry
                down
and open: No one there.   And suddenly, so naturally,
you are breathing not air but raw space. . . .

Ah, it's just as they say: the dead never know.
Things seem to go on exactly as they were,
the traffic, the pleasures, the ruckus of children,
though each year seems just a little shorter,
the seasons and subseasons in their sequence,
each with its little harvests and despairs,
a little more gettable, like the smooth braking
and acceleration out of a curve, and you sigh,
calling it wisdom, calling it skill with time.

You don't know which thoughts, now, you will never have
because you are dead. Just that less and less surprises you
in the still brutal and glorious and ordinary life
dreamed, now, completely in your head.
You don't imagine us still in the world you've phased out of,
our tears, our guilt at unwritten letters,
our poems in which you do not even know you are dead.

DEATH

He's not the Scyther, black hood, face in shadow;
still less the sinuous and cuff-linked Flourisher
of those cigarettes you can't buy anywhere;
and least of all the Seductress with a plan.
Since he dies repeatedly, Death has no experience.
When you meet, it might as well be his first time.
If there's a reason you should go, he's clueless.
If saintliness or subtlety of heart
in a universe just faintly just would save you,
he's much too young to understand,
but don't say that. Really he wasn't thinking
particularly of you, this teen with a too-big Uzi
he doesn't even know yet if he's going to use.

II.

HALF MEASURES

FIRSTCOMERS

Flowers that come early
may live low and pale
and in dense woods.
Trillium and violet
open before shade closes,
coolly thriving.

Daffodil and fern
in April, daring green,
must be bitter,
lest what is hungry, waking,
take them for what it dreamed of
all the hard winter.

DESIRE

I put my manic parakeet,
so cute I thought I would die,
in a box to keep it still,
and poured—was it love?—deep, deeply
into its flicking eyes.

O, desire is ingenious
and cruel, surely,
but how could I tell that boy,
little as he was, to *wait,* to *wait*—
for what, I cannot even now say clearly?

AGAIN

Really? Or did I dream
she passed my car in her car,
left-turning, gone.
Glass intervened, the huge
difference in our speeds:
as before.

PAUSED

I was climbing the crabapple's
frail and frailer branches,
almost too high,
awaiting the thought that would thin me
into sky.

I was rounding the marshy point
when I confused
sinewy wind in reeds
and froze,
snakeshy. All these years.

RECALL

Of all
my youth and freedom:
white December,
your white rooms
swallowing my calls
with a click-clack *You have reached* . . .
and then the number.

BOULDER

No lights, windows stony,
held breath of No One Home,
but there's a tilt of fox, I'm sure,
polarity of wing—

what was that tune,
the voice how in my head, sun
on which shoulder,
that would bring me in?

VALEDICTION

Something about the way you held your glass,
something about the way you set it down
firmly, and with a slight clockwise twist,
and didn't leave but, sitting an hour, found,

as if by accident, a way to be gone
strikes me: a bird's quick dark against the pane,
one word the wind brings, loud, from over the lake,
though *At last I know what you meant* is not what I mean.

HOUSE

Under a stone kicked over,
wrapped, I found a key,
though there was no house and no house
far as the eye could see.

Could Not

I cannot tell you what it was,
or how she said it.
My knees were freefall, and my glass
an outer planet.

I could not tell her that I heard
rain drying on the roof,
a shadow sharpening, a shovel's
harsh then *harsh* in gravel.

I was the cosmonaut,
all thrusters drained,
who tumbles (one last fry of static)
out of radio range.

Found

At my feet, this poem:
a Shaman, asked
Do these stones live?
glanced: *Some of them.*

Purpose

High in the tower
he built of cinder block,
our poor farmer,
wife dead a year,
got drunk enough to be one thing
and shot it.

Lunar

Any hunter-gatherer would know
which rodent it was, and where it vanished to,
hopping this little trail in the snow
that stops dead right beneath the moon.

Household Tips

You can get gum out of hair with peanut butter.
You can boost most cars with a letter opener,
replace lost tools with bent coathangers.

If your fingers sprout in the dark, wear a ring.
In the last week of the year,
write checks to the disasters you most fear.

Cliff

At last the air so steep
his breath,
clawing, clawing,
could not climb up.

Capital

The mind, an instrument of panic,
is most efficient closed
and blind as the bullet
the savior
at its gates is shot with
over and over.

E Pluribus Unum

From the stadium a surging
Ohhhhhh, and trailing . . .
Someone leaping for a pass
and thirty thousand falling . . .

Flock

Giddy, uproarious,
daughter and friends:
I feel as a tree must
when it can't tell its feelings
from the clamor of birds in its branches
suddenly lifting!

Any Port

Rain and a hot street
intersecting,
whiff of wet dust, tar,
a little like a harbor—
relief, by definition,
not what you were expecting.

Sparrows

Glint
in their dark eyes: door
to the next world
slightly ajar.

REUNION

In the aisle of relishes,
woman I haven't seen in thirty years.
I remember you so well, she says,
gazing somewhere in the air.

HISTORY

While you're trying to say
what happened,
some knots untie,
some tighten.

Those ants lifting
every lick
from a trap not
springing,

those empires falling,
pots
finally cooking,
while you're trying to say
what Time was:
Nobody Looking.

RELATIVISTIC EFFECTS

You head to work at lightspeed, over and over,
returning at evening for slow drinks
with that young man in the mirror.
But the songs escape you, and the girls,
your vehicle antique, your speech archaic burr.

THE CARDINALS

who peck at the faint (peck) bird in the pane:
who am I to say they never learn?

WRITER

When I waded through her cotton field
of balled paper
(this one I still call *little one),*
did my eyes water
because I was less alone, or lonelier?

THE BOOK OF EVERYTHING

In the time it takes to get down the page
from *It is a truth universally acknowledged*
to *You want to*
and *No cause, no cause*
the earth has turned you
just to where the horizon was.

ANCIENT

Sway of a daffodil, struggle of wings.
I warm
slowly (quickly) as a stone
just unshadowed by a cloud.
My fifty springs.

PARALLEL LINES

I calculate the reader's left to right
and down, and left to right again
through that novel's hundreds of years and pages
of trysts and catastrophes and talk
comes out to about a two-mile walk.

GRAVITAS

The fine chain lowered
in the dark well of your breasts,
the music gone soft,
the planet's
six sextillion tons
pulling the glass I easily
easily lift.

FORM

My two temptations
are one.
To be finished
And un-

RATIO OF VOLUME TO SURFACE AREA

Those skippers and silvers,
so tiny they have to land
on bright stones for warmth,
would freeze in your hand.

III.

VECTORS 2.0

More Aphorisms and Ten-Second Essays

1. Already tomorrow and too late, still yesterday and too soon.

2. Happiness, like water, is always available, but so often it seems we'd prefer a different drink.

3. The despair of the blank page: it is so full.

4. I don't see the curb well, so I drive way left, alarming the oncoming cars. How often fear makes us fearsome.

5. Ax built the house but sleeps in the shed.

6. *I have no time,* he snapped, as if he'd just asked himself for alms, and refused.

7. Birds of prey don't sing.

8. Fear the man who values his life. He will send you before him. Fear the man who doesn't. He will take you with him.

9. The chorus fills what the soloist has emptied.

10. I've spent so long trying to fly that it's too late to set out on foot.

11. The one who loves to hear himself talk isn't listening.

12. Mountains occur together.

13. Most of what looks like change is cliché perfecting itself.

14. Sun, I can't look at you. *That is why I shine.*

15. Institutions are the opposite of God: their periphery is everywhere, their center nowhere.

16. If the sky falls you get to see what's behind it.

17. When all agree, so does the Devil.

18. Was Midas turning the world into gold, or into himself? Either way, he starved.

19. Path: where nothing grows.

20. I envy music for being beyond words. But then, every word is beyond music.

21. Fire loves best what it cannot burn.

22. Yet sadly we feel that many of the noisiest are more interested in their indignation than in the injustice.

23. Water is weak, but it is water.

24. *First I have to learn to love myself,* always makes me writhe. I'm the last person I want to hear *I love you* from, the last I want to say it to. The part of myself I like is the part that works, like a good tool. The part of myself I love is the part that loves *you.*

25. The secret is a dream of someone it could be told to.

26. Some busy themselves to distract their passion, others because they cannot find it.

27. How often feelings are circular. How embarrassing to be embarrassed. How annoying to be annoyed.

28. When it's clear on Saturday, who notices? When it rains, it always does.

29. Hard to tickle or surprise myself, and if I make myself laugh it will be because I have become lost in trying to amuse others.

30. Travel reminds us we are always traveling.

31. So much of happiness is accidental that there are few rules for it. But one is: don't rule out accident.

32. Certain virtues assume distance. It is always someone else who is graceful or natural or wise. Even when it was myself.

33. Happiness is the readiness to be happy.

34. It's not a fact or feeling or even a flaw that's embarrassing, but who I was pretending to be.

35. In the first beautiful room we believe we are in Heaven. Once we have convinced ourselves we belong there, the flames.

36. I learn by finding out I was wrong to believe. But first I had to believe.

37. Lichtenberg says we don't blush in the dark because no one sees us. The crowd in my head can see in any light.

38. The most terrible book: all the things you were afraid to say to me.

39. I know your feelings with my feelings, but your thoughts I can hardly track. Maybe I deduce your motives, but even to you those are only like thoughts of thoughts.

40. No two flakes alike. Have they checked?

41. Listen to criticism: it reminds you what you were afraid to know. Don't listen too carefully: what you must do is something better than it knows how to say.

42. Never open the one with no return address. All the mass mailers know: the letter we think we want can't come from anyone.

43.   Better to repeat the obvious than fear it.

44.   Why do I complain, since I'd brush off solace? Some pains I just have to say, as if to confess faults before someone accuses me of them.

45.   What people say of us is no truer than what we say of ourselves. It only hurts more because we believe it.

46.   *Know thyself.* OK, so?

47.   I can "have" ideas or feelings or experiences, but I cannot really tell which are mine, and they can be given away freely. But some things I need permission to tell. Our real privacy belongs to others.

48.   How sure we are that everyone's watching. How sure we are that no one sees.

49.   It was not sin that brought death, but the reverse. When God first appeared in Eden, we started, suddenly ashamed we had a secret no immortal could understand.

50.   Apparently we were designed to be restrained by something above us. Why else would a little power or praise so regularly turn our brains, like suddenly uncapped sodas, to fizz?

51.   The Unembarrassable are like gods. We envy them; we hate them; they don't exist.

52.   I love sports. That there is an opponent! That there is an end! That someone wins! That there are reasons!

53.   Fandom is a relief from justice. Do we care how our team won, or whether they deserved to?

54.   The real danger of success is thinking you understand the reasons for it.

55. Would I give back all my undeserved failures if I also had to give back my undeserved successes?

56. My illness cures me. By telling me at last what's wrong.

57. *Injustice:* the god whose name we whisper when no other has remembered us.

58. No matter how much I lend it, life owes me nothing.

59. If you can't do what they want, you'll just have to do what you want.

60. Failure is freedom.

61. *What a fool!* I say of myself, with a vehemence and embarrassment that must mean I'd been thinking I wasn't.

62. Do not be too quick to pull out your flaws. They endure dry seasons, thrive uncared for. They have deeper roots than you. They hold the slope in place.

63. In saying my work fails I flatter myself that I have imagined what it should have been.

64. So many miracles that we only notice the ones that keep on not happening.

65. They break down my body, my peace, alas, my principles: demons are personal, like genes. They are the one-room fire on the 14th floor that crowds watch, glad it's someone else. For large-scale catastrophe, you need a god: something everyone believes in.

66. The wrong blessing is no blessing.

67. Beware the god who answers your prayers. He is recruiting.

68. The punishment of the faithless is to know their faithlessness. The punishment of the faithful is to believe in themselves. And all are punished by not knowing for sure which they are.

69. Whatever god wrote us is fond of characters who don't feel natural in their parts, who forget their lines.

70. A strength is a weakness in disguise.

71. Step back: the door out opens inwards.

72. It's not that no one notices his scam. It's just that it would be more tedious to expose him than to go along. Which is more annoying: that he doesn't know this, or that he probably does?

73. The only thing that uses up more energy than caring is trying not to.

74. He can't help being himself, I guess, but does he have to act like it?

75. I'm difficult to annoy, but the few who get the knack never seem to lose it.

76. Some things are too stupid even to be wrong.

77. His lie doesn't bother me as much as the truth he thinks he knows.

78. We trust the embarrassed one. He believes the world is thinking of him more than it is. But at least he believes in the world.

79. Games are for those who do not know they are games. Or for those who do. But they should not play together.

80. Useful to see how you could love every person, every job, for an hour. Necessary to realize how short an hour is.

81. I bought that to make it quiet. It's always silence we're buying.

82.   Maybe love has no limits, but we do.

83.   No one can do my job the way I do it. But lots of people do it fine another way.

84.   There is no misstep till you put your foot down.

85.   *There but for the grace of God go I.* We act as if we're saved repeatedly and by the merest accidents from turning into someone else. Whom we hate so we don't become him. Whom we love in case we do.

86.   When I swat the mosquito glutted with my blood, I fill with its smeared blackness.

87.   What scares me in suffering is the mechanical. The repetition compelled and wobbly, like a wheel with something wrong with it. The voice with something in it like bad brakes.

88.   The road you do not take you will have to cross.

89.   When we suffer, we think we owe nothing. We imagine we suffer so we can imagine we owe nothing.

90.   When I am free I cannot tell who is choosing for me. But the one struggling with chains is always myself.

91.   If you make rules only you can win by, they will play by other rules.

92.   Your lie is white only if you're sure you won't come to believe it.

93.   I think therefore I think again.

94.   Inside the head, art's not democratic. I wait a long time to be a writer good enough even for myself.

95.   If I have to make a decision, I'm not ready to.

96. A great deal of the world's trouble is caused by people who never make a mistake.

97. Indecision is excess of decision.

98. He Thought Positively till he became a euphemism for himself.

99. There is no road to the land without roads.

100. I haven't changed my mind. I just didn't know what it was.

101. Weather is predictable: it's timing that surprises.

102. The point isn't the point.

103. The thing that's hardest to remember about the past is how worried you were about this future.

104. With a new friend we change only a little. But a little.

105. When we say *I could not live without it* we mean *I would become someone else.* And we will.

106. A lot of people sound like the great poet. But she doesn't sound like them.

107. Zeitgeist. What everyone thinks everyone else is thinking.

108. Why should they love your work? Do you?

109. When I cook, I'm glad to have it taste just like at the restaurant. When I write, all I know is *That's not it.*

110. Only those who knew they were going to be rich can remember their poverty as freedom.

111.   As with bacteria, so with troubles. They evolve resistance to our cures.

112.   That others know: science. That others choose: politics.

113.   Superstorms, plagues, eco-crashes make us yearn for the century that feared Nature was indifferent. Now she is the lover we left, impoverished, powerfully intimate, vindictive.

114.   I sit by windows carelessly, as if no one were outside. I avoid mirrors, as if someone were in them.

115.   Solitude takes time. One becomes alone, like a towel drying, a stone warming.

116.   The loveliness of the bleak landscape, the stoic face. All they have allowed us to feel for ourselves.

117.   The water cannot talk without the rocks.

118.   I only like being the center of the universe when no one else is there.

119.   If we walked in the sky it would not be the sky.

120.   Statistics says: in your glass of cool water there are molecules hotter than the surface of a star.

121.   The stones, the rays outnumber us. Do not ask the universe for a vote.

122.   I think of my memory as weakening, but, no, only my power of using it has declined. It was once like a library that existed only for me—I'd send someone down for a fact. The facts are still there, but my gofer gets lost. The books are reshelving themselves, reshuffling their pages, growing together. They have their own plan, and there is nothing to do but learn to read it.

123.   He overestimates everyone. Is that modesty or unwillingness to help?

124.   It's never my own wizened, harried, scared youth I want back, and I don't really know how to wish for anyone else's. It's not a younger body I need, though soon I may. It's Time, I say, I want more Time. But I always feel that most strongly when I'm wasting it on busyness, sterility and boredom—when I can't even use what I've got. *Ah, youth!* means *Why can't I live?*

125.   Who had to beg owes you nothing.

126.   I shot a bird once, through the head. I dove from a thirty foot cliff, just once, into waters I hadn't checked. And once I walked out on a life. Now these things seem less possible than the Impossible. Just because I did them doesn't mean I'm capable of them, or even that I was.

127.   He welcomes rain who wants to stay home.

128.   Tree's most tree when it tries to run.

129.   If you could fall forever it would be the same as freedom.

130.   Innocence is not a state; it is each of us. Experience is our disagreement. If I met my double, we could convince each other any fantastic thing was real, and who knows what would happen.

131.   I worked so hard to understand it that it must be true.

132.   What modesty or piety or evasion makes us think first *Save the children?* Why should their deaths be more horrible than their parents', unless in quiet despair we are really thinking *Kill me but not my unlived life, take me but not my time?*

133.   Judge them, if you must, by what they settled for. But do not mistake it for what they imagined.

134.   The hardest thing to allow my child is my mistakes.

135.   I was 25 till I was 40, 40 till I was 50. But now my age is like the speedometer. If I don't pay attention it drifts, 60, 70, 80 . . .

136.   Over and over I find I'm too credulous to be wise, too ready to believe myself, and also the one who tells me not to.

137.   Soon you will throw this day away, if you haven't already lost it.

138.   Wisdom was . . . knowing how to hold your head in the wind. But hold it that way always and you're a sermon, an ad, an idiot.

139.   The lonelier the road the more creatures you startle.

140.   Each year gets late earlier.

141.   Since nothing clichés more readily than desire, art is always trying to find something it did not know it wanted.

142.   Those who worked like dogs, those who dogged it, those who screwed up, those who made all the right moves, those who didn't move at all: here we all are.

143.   Already the world needs saving that I saved yesterday.

144.   Light, the Beasts of the Field, the Firmament: easy. But not till the seventh day did God figure out Rest.

145.   You can go get what you want, but you'll have to wait for life to bring you what you didn't know you wanted.

146.   All the truths have been said, but which of them are true?

147.   Save me, O Lord, from waiting to be saved.

148.   Billions of years, the dust hasn't settled. Water's still seeking its own level.

149.   There is no last line we don't have to go beyond.

150.   A car or stone becomes the exact temperature of the winter, but a man gets colder and colder.

IV.

LATECOMERS

EARLY SNOW

Let a bleak paleness chalk the door
So all within be livelier than before.
                              —Herbert

If I could make leaves, I'd surely want to keep them,
but forests let whole summers of them fall,
parting that must come easier, come autumn
when their spring green looks a little worse for wear.

It's economical. In temperate modern climes
replacement runs you much less than repair,
and broad, flat leaves, perfect for catching sun,
also catch snow, backbreaking megatons.

We saw that once, vistas of oak and maple
beheaded by a heavy September snow,
millions of refugees streaming to the horizon,
bent double carrying everything they owned.

Some landing, miles-wide jet had shaved them level,
some charless blast had evanesced their crowns,
exposing the full-dress leafage of our summer
as a nakedness, battered, steaming under snow—

moment of impact when you can't tell what is broken,
instant, waking, you don't know who is gone,
our pale pale friend rehabbing from a stroke,
More years than you have, just to get back where you were.

Where were we? On the Taghkanic. Eighty-something.
All that was shattered, surely, has regrown.
Our daughters are gone. As for the first snow,
it was probable weeks, it was possible years ago.

229

Is this it? The faint blur at the end of sight,
the ticking on the pane, that missed stair in the chest?
So many times we've whispered, *This is it.*
Well, it's December. Once we will be right.

Already the schoolkids cheer for it to mount
into the little disaster they call freedom,
nowhere to go but everywhere,
that feeling *Nothing to lose* so quickly lost—

help me to hold it! As for our list
of Have, of Should, of Probably Never Will
or Really Never Wanted Enough to Do
and Didn't: drop it and grow again.

Let snows obliterate the walks and roads
and all our lots blend lightly into one.
Better by far the cold of the gods should kill us
than their gifts, or that we would not let them go.

LATECOMERS

Never my mother told me *drive through piles of leaves.*
There might be children. . . .

*

The dark at four, that too-soon
bending for a low door,
that driving fast
to get home while the car, a held breath,
lasts.

*

Skidmarks, guardrail down.
Some crazy pod has blown
like frost-breath, like the foam
where Ceres' daughter,
kiss-strong, plunged her chariot
through the black earth as if it were water.

*

Under the ocean
of new dark, our little house,
a slide held up to the light.
Don't open
windows, lest our lamps,
lest in our minds
the dime-size skies,
be doused.

*

Downed line crackling, misdelivered bill
that the lateness of the year makes into Signs.
Four leaves, yellow:
Yield, O Yield.

*

Crest of a hill,
the still-reorganizing air
where something left through something like a door.

And looking down,
the postal depot's hundred vans
setting out on their appointed rounds,
rays of a great white flower.

*

That bending forward when the car,
for a sudden yellow, brakes.
That straightening up
in whatever the opposite is of prayer.

*

The god who thought of all the other gods,
who doesn't need us to believe:
so slowly was it built, his Cathedral
of the Empty Fields,
ironweed and goldenrod
its waste metals,
that it fades slowly.

You can still hear it,
the faint roar of height
in the ears of the stone carvers

way up, small as sparrows,
and the click of their chisels
as crickets, crickets.

*

Flicker (suppressed) of recognition,
rolling his window down—
as if he might be my Fate
asking (ironically) for directions,

or I might be his.
Muting my music,
I tell him how the streets turned
in the universe as I used to know it.

*

The lingering touch on your shoulder, wave to UPS,
the sounding interested in whoever drops by the office,
telepathic aid to the kid with the heavy backpack,
this sitting here watching how squirrels
bury things shallowly all over, these little winds
scattering our seeds so widely that when winter comes
it won't be able to find us in all the size of our land.

*

The cardoor-slam, steps in the gravel, keys.
(Are we all home?)
Someone returning, late
thousands of years, only to ask what's happened,
breath of wet stone.

*

House is a tree
we climb in, sleeping
at the tip of a branch, upstairs,
TV left on
to discourage predators.

*

Is it late or early?
Some party breaking up,
knots of hilarity.
Doors slamming
and slamming harder.
Apparently the hi-beams
see nothing
in our dark room, lit,
then darker.

*

On their stoops,
mothers with the same wood spoon
calling in unison
children who will turn over
to sleep all winter, or rise,
arms out like scarecrows,
leaves streaming down their sides.

EARLY AND LATE

Pure wintry poise, the abstract trees and skies
of the first leafless day, when finally
you see it: freedom and desolation.
Like the fight in which everything comes out,
our lives untwining almost to the last
loose end. Think Michelangelo,
Titans allegorically suspended
forefinger to forefingertip.
Invisible the lightning between them
that binds the Universe, striking both up and down.
Who, then, who can tell Divine from Human?
Change pours, the sun turns on in both heads,
trees light and shed, lakes crack:
Creation and Abandonment
in one instant, or, in the other version,
Dreaming a God and Falling . . .

IN SNOW

The snow is smoothing down a life-size map
on what it is a map of, losing some detail
in the service of overview.

How even-handed is its sympathy
for hardening stream and softening stone,
how fine-grained its attention
to white lawns, whitening roads,
and roofs, gray black or tan, gone monotone.

*

Steeper and steeper, the dream canyon
I labor at the bottom of,
the thousand feet of snow
I've shoveled all these years from the drive,
clouds at cloud-height barely scraping over,
sparrows at their apogee, just over.

*

Coolly and kindly it resolves
our little difficulty with time,
pausing the mail, the schools,
in a kind of video loop, showing more and more
of what falls and lifts in the wind, refalling whiter and slower.

*

Whiter and darker,
white earth I tunnel through.
Deeper than the house, below the laws,
like a little light at the bottom of a lake,

is a window.
Someone at a brass fire rubs his hands.
Mind snows
around an image he cannot let go:

deeper down,
love, you are loose
in a huge summer, dreaming
how once you slept
on a white altar,
azure snowlight your brow.

*

dust from what saw

time

rushing to explain
by saying *again and again*

*

The azure of your wrists, your sighs
and the stairs they climb,
the faint, sure rising of the moon
behind your azure lids.

Hills still blue in snow,
blue pines.
The dogear in my *Life of . . .*
is a waterline:

Never higher than here.

*

White drifts, white brows.

Two houses or two friends
who have not said a thing for hours,
agreeing (maybe it's the wine)
on everything everything.

The sky not letting on it's coming down.

*

Flashes and floaters.
In the basement, even, glint of waters.
Faint flocks in the dead of winter.

Anywhere we lie down
(but O, how fall'n),
is bed of the ancient sea.

In the periphery of vision
Permian creatures,
sand fine as snow
in the shoes you haven't worn for eons.

*

So the leaves are not going to fall.
Time's past when it was easier to make new ones
than suffer damage to the old.
So few years to the end of the world
now, three or four,
that we'll stick with what we have
and spend
desires, reserves,

leave all lamps on all night
and all the stars.

Windows thrown open,
heat rolling out,
voluminous our frost-breath,
snow steaming off our brows,

our bodies hollowing,
eyes fever-bright,
like moths that do not eat
once in their whole moth-lives.

*

It's all awake in the snow! Tulips, icy roses,
full-leaved maples, frost-slicked swallowtails,
beauty so cold, so frail
it pains, so true.
Birds of mid-summer, languorous slow-openers,
snow-touched, unreproved,
snow melding with the aqua swimming pools.

Children circling drifted-over picnics,
excited, snow
subliming on their outstretched arms, their hair.
The sideslice of their Frisbees through the sleet,
snared
with rose-warm rose-cold hands,
and the long returns expiring
like contrails in the upper air.

*

Snow snowing
into the volume open on your lap,
suffusing earlier and later pages.

Curtains of vapor
where you slip in quietly,
shocking the pool white.

*

the static
under the picture
under the static

covering up its fall
with falling

when you can't speak
because the sound's turned off

back of every photograph

*

The way we hear
under white ice the toiling waters,

the way we are
characters in two different novels
meeting in what reader,

the way you feel,
your hand pressed flat, the snow
ticking and streaming on the warm-cold window.

EVENING PRAYER

How can we blame you for what we have made of you,
war, panic, rulings, desperate purity?
Who can blame us? Lord knows, we are afraid of time,
terrible, wonderful time, the only thing not yours.
Granted, we heard what we wanted to hear,
were sentenced, therefore, to our own strange systems
whose main belief was that we should believe.

You, of course, are not religious, don't need any rules
that can be disobeyed, have no special people,
and since a god, choosing (this the myths got right),
becomes human, avoided choices
in general, which is why there is Everything,
even imagination, which thinks it imagines
what isn't, an error you leave uncorrected.

The rumor you were dead, you, I think,
suggested, letting us go with only *Pray*
into what you had made. By which you meant,
I know, nothing the divine accountants
could tote up on their abaci *click click,*
but to widen like a pupil in the dark.
To be a lake, on which the overhanging pine,
the late-arriving stars, and all the news of men,
weigh as they will, are peacefully received,
to hear within the silence not quite silence
your prayer to us, *Live kindly, live.*

ANOTHER END OF THE WORLD

Here in the last minutes, the very end of the world,
someone's tightening a screw thinner than an eyelash,
someone with slim wrists is straightening flowers,
someone is starting a slow, cloud-like settling
into a love longer than the world,
and someone's playing chess. Chess!
Some can't believe how little time is left,
some have been counting down the seconds
in pennies, all their lives. And one has realized
this day was made for him, seeing nothing
he had to do needs to be done,
and whistles, hands in pockets. This is how the world begins.

LATE SNOW

There's always a chance it won't like stopping,
will warm to the idea of going on and on
through April, to see for itself what's happening
beyond the yellow walls of daffodils,
and what May's like, that hour it has never stayed up till.
Will beg to be allowed to watch from a distance
the rumor of June, that afterland, July,
will be flexible to get what it wants, conceding
even on temperature and color
to snow warmly and invisibly
over your short-sleeved guests in August,
a slight dilution of their upheld wine.
It promises to be good, will moderate
its obsession with the hexagon
and tendency to drift, until at last
it can't be told from the stiffness of your rising,
a little late, in the latter days of summer,
from the dry clear downpour of the sun,
from your dream of the early snow still weeks and weeks in the future.

INTERGLACIAL

Anyone's story,
dear, ours:
almost didn't happen.
One
incredible day
between two colds.
The *"O and . . . "*
someone out the door
leaned back in to say. . . .

EPILOGUE IN SNOW

The distant speck I'm taking as my model
of a man who wastes time well might say
whose woods these are, if they're not mine,
but he swerves, as I also swerve, away.

I watch the woods fill up with road, or snow;
and snow, or woodland, overflow the road.
The wind has whited out the signs
that would say who owns what's next, if anyone.

NOTES & ACKNOWLEDGMENTS

The title, *Interglacial,* means "occurring between glacial epochs."

Reservations (Princeton University Press, 1977) was originally dedicated to John, *Second Guesses* (Wesleyan University Press, 1984) to Connie and Connie. *As If* (Persea Books/National Poetry Series, 1992) was for Kate, L.C., Julie, Ted, and Connie, *How Things Are* (Carnegie Mellon University Press, 2000) for Catherine W. Richardson, and *Vectors* (Ausable Press, 2001) again for Connie. The "Afterword" to "How Things Are" is from *A Suite for Lucretians* (Quarterly Review of Literature Poetry Series, 1999). "The Encyclopedia of the Stones" was originally dedicated to Samuel H. Monk. The version printed here is earlier and shorter than the one in *Reservations.* "Marigolds" was dedicated to H. M. B., "How Things Are: A Suite for Lucretians" to Ted Weiss, "Through Autumn" to Connie.

Thanks to the editors of the publications in which parts of the final section, "Interglacial: New Poems and Aphorisms," have previously appeared:

AGNI—"Latecomers," "Frictions"
Barrow St.—"Any Port," "Purpose," 25 aphorisms
Boulevard—"Early Snow"
The Formalist—"Form"
Kelsey Review—"Reunion," "Desire," "Flock"
Lilliput Review—"Gravitas"
Paris Review—"All the Ghosts"
Saint Ann's Review—"Valediction"
Slate—"My Godzilla," "Still Life with Moving Figure," "Spellbound"
U.S. 1 Worksheets—"Could Not," "SF"
Yale Review—"In Black and White," 49 Aphorisms

Special thanks to Gerald Costanzo for many kindnesses over the past few years, and particularly for permission to include so much of *How Things Are,* which is still in print.

I'm grateful for the timely assistance of a 2001-2002 Artists Fellowship from the New Jersey State Council on the Arts and a 2002 Award in Literature from the American Academy of Arts and Letters.

Dozens of Friend Points go to Paul Muldoon, David Orr, and Carolyn Williams, who read a version of this manuscript, and hundreds go to Chase Twichell and Connie Hassett, who put up with multiple versions and with the poet himself.

*

"Anyway," the floating introductory poem, belongs in *As If*.

"As One Might Have Said." If one were . . . Hopkins?

"Essay on Birds." It's most likely that migrating birds navigate using the sun and the earth's magnetic field, but they may also get help from the stars, ultraviolet, and perhaps ultra low-frequency sounds (produced by, among other things, the oceans), which can be heard at great distances.

"Doppler Effects." The familiar rise and fall of the pitch of a train whistle as it approaches, then recedes. Analogously, the light of approaching objects is blueshifted, that of fleeing objects redshifted. The poem assumes, impossibly, that the universe reaches the limit of its expansion at the mid-point of my life, and that when it begins contracting time runs backwards.

"Out of the Sun." Fungoes are fly balls hit for outfield practice. "Shagging . . . flies" is chasing them down. A Zero was a World War II Japanese fighter plane.

"Compositae." Composites (e.g. daisies, dandelions, thistles), so-called because the central head contains many tiny flowers, are the largest family of flowering plants. Wild Carrot, not a composite, is another name for Queen Anne's Lace (snap the root and smell it).

"At First, at Last." To put it too simply, the anthropic principle says that the nature of the universe is oddly dependent on us: if it were very different, we would never have evolved to observe it.

"How Things Are: A Suite for Lucretians." Section 1: Long Island, land of my youth, is a New York suburb (and actually, as I learned too late for this poem, produces some pretty decent wines). Section 17: the shuffling of wind and light and cloud is a little homage to Swinburne's great poem "By the North Sea," which everyone must read right away. Section 22: the thinning ring is a famous Lucretian image, as is the plowshare diminishing in the fields, though I have shifted the latter towards "sheer plod makes plow down sillion shine," from Hopkins' "The Windhover."

"Salvage." In the 70's a dead giraffe was scooped out of New York harbor. Think about it.

"Letter from One of Many Worlds." An incredibly crude version of the "many worlds interpretation of quantum mechanics" would go something like this: when you come to a fork in the road, the universe itself branches; in one universe you take the left fork, in the other, the right.

"The Water as it Was." The Verrazano is a bridge between Staten Island and Brooklyn.

"The Dreaming-Back." After death, according to Yeats in *A Vision,* "the Spirit is compelled to live over and over again the events that had most moved it."

"Poison." "Bluestone" is a name for, among other things, copper sulfate crystals and driveway gravel.
"A Disquisition upon the Soul." The exposure time of Victorian film was so long that a pedestrian, say, could pass between the camera and its subject and leave no trace in the final photograph.

"Mothy Ode" travesties a bit of Keats's "Ode to a Nightingale" and a lot of Shelley's "Hymn of Apollo."

"Through Autumn." Section 20: for an object the size of a bacterium the force of Brownian motion (the random bumping of water molecules) is far greater than gravity. There is no "down." Section 28: "proprioception" is the body's sense of its movement and orientation. Section 30: cabbage whites (often called "cabbage moths," though they're not moths) are those white butterflies you often see in little flocks.

"Monster Movies." "Serpent that rings the planet": in Norse mythology, the evil Jormungand encircles the world, biting its own tail. "Green knight:" from *Sir Gawain and the Green Knight.* Boys of a certain generation will remember that Superman had a secret identity, was vulnerable to Kryptonite and built his "Fortress of Solitude" in the Arctic. Certain details of the poem may be clearer to those who have seen the sci-fi movie *Independence Day,* but don't rush out.

"Still Life with Moving Figure." Mike Donohue tells me that it was, indeed, a *Twilight Zone*, but I haven't checked to see how many of the details I've misremembered.

"SF." Fans will recognize that the landscape owes something to the far-far-future Earth of Gene Wolfe's *The Book of the New Sun.* "Zeptosecond" is not yet in the dictionary, but science wants it to mean "one sextillionth of a second."

"Death." The Uzi is a submachine gun of Israeli manufacture.

"Could Not" is bounced off Christina Rossetti's "May."

"The Book of Everything." The first two italicized phrases are from *Pride and Prejudice,* the third from *King Lear.*
"Gravitas." "Six sextillion tons" is the weight of the Earth.

"Ratio of Volume to Surface Area." Skippers and silvers are very small butterflies. Tiny creatures (little volume, relatively large surface area) lose body heat easily.

"Early Snow." "Help me to hold it" is borrowed from Robert Browning's "Two in the Campagna." I don't really know if it was the 70's or 80's, September or October, but anyway millions of trees still in leaf had their tops snapped off by a heavy snow. The Taghkanic or Taconic Parkway heads north from New York.